PETRARCH
SELECTED POEMS

Petrarch

SELECTED POEMS

TRANSLATED INTO ENGLISH BY
Anthony Mortimer

THE UNIVERSITY OF ALABAMA PRESS
University, Alabama

Library of Congress Cataloging in Publication Data

Petrarca, Francesco, 1304–1374.
  Petrarch : selected poems.

  Bibliography: p.
  Includes index.
  I. Mortimer, Anthony Robert.
PQ4496.E23M6   851'.1   76-54222
ISBN 0-8173-8526-6

CONTENTS

ACKNOWLEDGMENTS

Work on these translations began in 1970 when, as an exchange-visitor from Britain, I was teaching English and Comparative Literature at Case Western Reserve University. My first thanks, therefore, must go to all the friends and colleagues who helped to make my stay pleasant and productive. James Taaffe and Roger Salomon were generous with their advice and hospitality. Peter Salm gave me the benefit of his own experience as a translator. Sarah DeVenne, then a graduate student, made an unfailingly patient listener and sacrificed her own work to forward mine. My greatest debt is to Hugh Amory, who read every single version with an attention worthy of better things. The failings that remain have certainly not escaped his criticism, but I hope that he will recognize his own hand in some of the happier moments. Among my colleagues at the University of Geneva, George Steiner provided some brief yet crucial suggestions, and Andrew Joscelyne gave a fresh and perceptive reading to my final revision.

There is enough Petrarchan scholarship to keep one busy for a lifetime, but at least three works have proved indispensable: the Carducci-Ferrari edition of the *Rime* (Florence, 1899), Ernest Hatch Wilkins' *The Making of the Canzoniere* (Rome, 1951), and Umberto Bosco's exemplary monograph, *Francesco Petrarca* (Bari, 1946).

Finally, if I have not included any discussion of Wyatt and the Tudor Petrarchists, this is only because I have already dealt with them in my recent book, *Petrarch's Canzoniere in the English Renaissance* (Bergamo and Milan, 1975).

Geneva, August, 1975   A.M.

INTRODUCTION

To the book of poems that we now know as the *Canzoniere* or the *Rime* Petrarch gave the title *Rerum vulgarium fragmenta*. We should not, however, be misled by the somewhat deprecatory attitude that this title suggests. The great Latinist of the prose works, the *Epistolae metricae*, and the epic *Africa* was anything but casual in his approach to the vernacular lyrics. Although the opening sonnet seems to dismiss the "scattered rhymes" as the product of an erring youth, we know that Petrarch was still working on the *Canzoniere* a few months before his death at the age of seventy. Nor was this simply a question of adding poems to the collection or editing those already written. As recent scholarship has shown, the *Canzoniere* evolved through a long and arduous process of ordering, selection, and revision amounting at times to recomposition. So thorough was Petrarch's preparation of the final manuscript (Vatican MS. 3195) that it becomes extremely difficult, on stylistic evidence alone, to call any of the poems youthful or mature. Even a sonnet originally composed as early as 1330 may have been radically revised thirty or forty years later. The stylistic and tonal unity of the *Canzoniere* is so great that we cannot speak of development without recourse to manuscript evidence. In the *Canzoniere* as we have it there is no early or late Petrarch, but only the one unchanging Petrarch presented by the poet himself in the traditional framework of a love story.

The story itself is simple. It tells how, on April 6, 1327, the poet saw a girl called Laura in the church of St. Clare in Avignon. For twenty-one years he loved her with alternating hope and despair, joy and sorrow. In 1348 she died on the exact anniversary of their first meeting. For ten more years he continued to cherish her image, still fluctuating and torn between grief at her death and hope that she would

1

guide him to join her in Paradise. Finally, renouncing all earthly affections, he turned his thoughts wholly to God. The bald outline may not tell us much about the real distinction of the *Canzoniere*, but it does indicate Petrarch's reliance on traditions established by the three preceding schools of love poetry: the Provençal, the Sicilian, and the Dolce Stil Novo. Love at first sight, the contrasting aspects of the lover's state, the remarkable coincidence of dates, the lady as a guide to heaven, the final renunciation—none of these is original in Petrarch. With the exception of the renunciation, we can find them all in Dante's *Vita Nuova*. And even the renunciation had been fixed by Andreas Capellanus as a recognized part of the convention. The debt to tradition is no less obvious when we look at things in more detail. The praise of the lady as a perfect work of God and Nature, her golden hair, white skin, perfect hand, and slender fingers, the splendor of her smile, the sweetness of her greeting, her lover's fear that she may be dead or that he may have offended her, his awkward silence in her presence, his longing for solitude, his visions and memories—we may call these Petrarchan conventions only so far as Petrarch passed them on to the Renaissance. They were already conventions when he used them.

Why then is the *Canzoniere* so important? Or, to put it another way, what distinctive poetic vision emerges through the conventional framework? De Sanctis, with characteristic force, gives the answer that has since become a cliché:

> The reader of the *Canzoniere* cannot fail to receive the impression of an abstract, rhetorical, sophistical world, like that displayed by the troubadours, but with sentiments more human and real and forms more clear and defined; or, if we care to look higher, a mystico-scholastic, ultra-human world, still accepted by the intellect, but rejected by the heart and condemned by the imagination. . . . The Gothic church has been transformed into a lovely little Greek temple, nobly decorated, elegant, with equal light, with perfect symmetry, inspired by Venus, goddess of beauty and grace.[1]

[1] Francesco De Sanctis, *Storia della letteratura italiana*, in *Opere*, ed. Niccolò Gallo (Milan and Naples, 1961), p. 265.
Chi legge il Canzoniere, non può non ricevere questa impressione, di un mondo

The *Canzoniere* is thus made to exemplify the transition from the spiritual, Christian Middle Ages to the sensuous, pagan Renaissance. And De Sanctis, as a good nineteenth-century liberal, makes no secret of his preference for the latter. The *Canzoniere* is seen as an advance from the abstract, symbolic system of the Scholastics into an increasingly human world. The allegorized Beatrice of Dante is contrasted with Petrarch's "real" Laura and her "definite woman's personality." It is a "human body" and not an abstraction that now warms the poet's imagination.

The whole interpretation, of course, leans heavily on a Burckhardtian view of the period. We are given a Petrarch caught between the divine and the human, the spiritual and the sensual. But can this really be seen as a sign of the times and a condition peculiar to Petrarch? Let us go back a century and consider for a moment that manifesto of the Dolce Stil Novo, Guido Guinizelli's *Al cor gentil ripara sempre Amore*. We are told that as God, through the angels, informs and directs the heavens with his creating will, so the beauty of the lady, acting through the eyes of the lover, disposes him to obedience and spiritual elevation. In the last stanza, however, the poet imagines himself reproved by God for having compared human and divine love. He replies: "She bore the semblance of an angel from your kingdom; it was no fault of mine if I loved her."[2] The conclusion is a self-justification, but it also implies an admission that, in the absolute light of eternity, the comparison between God and the lady cannot be maintained. Only in Dante do we get a convincing

astratto, rettorico, sofistico, quale fu foggiato da' trovatori, dove appariscono sentimenti più umani e reali e forme più chiare e rilevate, o se vogliamo guardare più alto, di un mondo mistico-scolastico, oltreumano, ammesso ancora dall' intelletto, ma repulso dal cuore e condannato dall'immaginazione . . . il tempio gotico si è trasformato in un bel tempietto greco, nobilmente decorato, elegante, con luce uguale, con perfetta simetria, ispirato da Venere, dea della bellezza e della grazia.
All translations in the text are my own.
   [2] *Dir li potrò: tenea d'angel sembianza*
   che fosse del tu' regno;
   non mi fu fallo, s'eo li posi amanza.

resolution of this problem. When we look elsewhere we are forced to recognize that the tension between sacred and profane love is an integral part of the tradition that Petrarch inherited.

It is not only on historical grounds that one can quarrel with De Sanctis. He speaks of a "definite woman's personality," but we seek it in vain in the *Canzoniere* which tells us little about Laura except that she is the object of the poet's love. Her actions, if indeed she can be said to act, conform almost totally to the conventional ideal of ineffable courtesy and unconquerable virtue. Nor is Petrarch's love of the sensual kind that De Sanctis might lead us to expect. In the sestina *A qualunque animale alberga in terra* (XXII) we do get a flash of physical desire when the poet longs to spend a night with his mistress; but this is the exception rather than the rule. The phrases used to describe Laura's physical presence — "golden tresses," "fair limbs," "angelic breast" — are too automatic for eroticism and too vague for the convincing portrayal of a truly "human body." What is true of Laura is true of Petrarch's imagery in general. There is more sense of physical reality in one canto of the *Divine Comedy* than in the whole of the *Canzoniere*.

We have not, however, been quoting De Sanctis only to reject him. He is too perceptive a critic not to have left us with some clue to the real nature of the *Canzoniere*. Having spoken of Laura's "definite woman's personality" and of Petrarch's love for her "human body," he goes on to make a significant modification.

> You might say that Laura is a model with whom the painter has fallen in love, not as a man, but as a painter, intent less on possessing than on representing her. And Laura is, indeed, little more than a model, a lovely serene form, placed there to be contemplated and depicted, a pictorial creature.[3]

[3] De Sanctis, p. 251.
Diresti Laura un modello, del quale il pittore sia innamorato, non come uomo, ma come pittore, intento meno a possederlo che a rappresentarlo. E Laura è poco più che un modello, una bella forma serena, posta lì per essere contemplata e dipinta, creatura pittorica.

Laura is essentially an object of contemplation, an aesthetic vision; not one term in the contrast of flesh and spirit, but hovering in between, equally threatened by both those non-aesthetic truths, the temporal concrete truth of the senses and the eternal abstract truth of religion.

We need not go so far as Petrarch's friend, Giacomo Colonna, who suggested that the real object of the poet's desire was not Laura at all, but the poetic laurel that she personified. Petrarch insisted on the real existence of Laura and we have no cause to question his honesty. But this real Laura leaves little trace in the *Canzoniere*. The Laura that wakes the lyricism of Petrarch is rarely present to his physical eye; she is evoked from the past, projected into the future, re-created in absence, always transformed into aesthetic object. The sonnet *Erano i capei d'oro a l'aura sparsi* (XC) is a notable example. The appearance of Laura on some past occasion is recalled in terms that clearly derive from the apparition of Venus in Book One of the *Aeneid*. The past is evoked, not with the remembered evidence of the senses, but with literary allusions that have a mythic resonance. We recognize that this vision is a fragile creation, constantly threatened by hard facts and creeping doubts. Laura's eyes no longer have their old radiance; the look of pity that the poet once saw may never have been there. But these unwelcome thoughts are soon submerged in a flood of assertion:

> She moved not like a mortal, but as though
> she bore an angel's form; her words had then
> a sound that simple human voices lack;
>
> a heavenly spirit, a living sun,
> was what I saw; now, if it is not so,
> the wound's not healed because the bow grows slack.

The wound is more enduring than the bow, the effect more vital than the cause. The real Laura, recognized and dismissed in the penultimate line, is less compelling than the poetic image she has inspired. Petrarch is not a Pygmalion who falls

5

in love with the statue and prays that it be endowed with breath and motion. The process is quite the reverse. The moving, breathing creature can only be truly loved and happily contemplated when held and transformed in the fragile stasis of art.

A similar transformation is worked upon the landscape which is so often a background for the poet's meditations or a setting for the figure of Laura. Much has been written about Petrarch's love of nature, and certainly the letters give ample evidence that he was genuinely sensitive to the beauty of his home in Vaucluse. Yet the *Canzoniere* has little in the way of detailed natural description. Sometimes, as in the two great canzoni, CXXVI and CXXIX, we get the impression that a landscape has been described, but it remains obstinately difficult to visualize. We may almost feel cheated at finding that our landscape has been created from such simple material as "high mountains," "wild woods," "shadowed vale," "green grass," and "white cloud." The nouns are generic and the adjectives obviously fitting rather than strikingly accurate. We may look for the details of a specific landscape, but we find only the basic elements from which a landscape may be composed. We are given a sense of atmosphere, not a sense of place.

The fact is that a precisely described natural scene would prove destructive of Petrarch's careful artifact which must always exist at a certain distance from the world of concrete phenomena. Petrarch's gift is the capacity to simplify a landscape down to its essential components, which, deprived of their independent objective existence, can be manipulated, transformed, and rebuilt into a personal aesthetic vision. Just because Petrarch is no nature mystic, his artifact is too fragile to support the weight of concrete observed phenomena. He does not have Wordsworth's confidence in a subjective vision which can transform even the smallest details of a natural scene into facets of a mental landscape.

The reader should not be surprised to find me, at this stage, using the words "vision" and "artifact" almost as synonyms. In the poem *Di pensier in pensier* (CXXIX) the poet avoids the company of men and retreats to uninhabited nature because only there, in solitude, can he build his artifact without disturbance. On the first stone he mentally forms the face of Laura; he sees her image in the water, in the grass, in the trunk of a beech, and in a passing cloud. The more deserted the scene, the more effective the transformation becomes. Yet even here it takes an effort to maintain the vision. There always comes the moment "when the truth removes that sweet illusion" and when the stone is once again a stone. The vision has been recognized as no more than an artifact. Constantly seduced by the creations of his own poetic imagination, the poet realizes that they cut him off from the true image, *l'imagine vera*. He knows that the visionary stasis is dangerously unsubstantial in that it involves a suspension of normal human perception in a world governed by time and mutability. His most ecstatic moments of contemplation are veined by the melancholy knowledge that he is, in fact, *carco d'oblio* or, as Wyatt puts it, "charged with forgetfulness."

Let us look at another example. In the fourth stanza of *Chiare fresche e dolci acque* (CXXVI) we get what is surely one of the most attractive pictures in the Petrarchan gallery. Laura sits upon the grass and the flowers rain down upon her, some catching in her hair, some resting in her lap:

> Some, sweetly turning through the air,
> Seemed in their drift to whisper: "Love reigns here."

With these lines the vision, earlier described as "sweet in the memory," seems to have become present again. In the pause between stanzas we remain rapt in admiration. The final stanza, however, brings back the mood of uncertainty and the nagging sense of illusion.

> How often I exclaimed,
> seized by a sudden fear,
> "For certain she was born in Paradise!"

Such deep oblivion came
from her celestial air,
the words, the gentle smiling, and the eyes,
so faintly did I seize
the image truth would show,
that I said sighing then:
"How came I here, or when?"
thinking myself in heaven, not here below.
And ever since I've loved this place
so much that elsewhere I can find no peace.

Song, had you beauty as you have desire,
intrepidly you could
go out among the crowd and leave this wood.

It is not Petrarch's intention to bring us down to earth with a
bump. The vision is flawed, but not shattered; and the poet's
last regret is not for having surrendered to illusion, but for
having been unable to present that illusion in its full beauty.
The Petrarchan vision can be neither long sustained nor long
abandoned. The result is that complex interaction of con-
trasting emotions and attitudes so often seen as characteristic
of Petrarch, but never better described than in the words of
Umberto Bosco:

> Love, in this most celebrated of Petrarch's love poems (*CXXVI*), is
> born directly from contemplative bliss, which is often one with the
> joy of day-dreaming, and which is rendered intimate by the poet's
> self-pitying introspection. In this alternation and fusion of outward
> and inward turning, of surrender to the dream and return to the self
> in elegiac meditation, consists perhaps the nucleus from which
> springs, in its concrete realization, the lyric strength of Petrarch.[4]

[4] Umberto Bosco, *Francesco Petrarca* (Bari, 1961), p. 36.
*L'amore, in questo celeberrimo tra i canti petrarcheschi d'amore, nasce dunque
propriamente da gaudio contemplativo, che è spesso tutt'uno con la gioia del
fantasticare, e al quale conferisce intimità il ripiegare del poeta su se stesso, per
commiserarsi. In questo alternarsi e fondersi dell'espandersi e del rientrare,
dell'abbandonarsi al sogno e del riprendersi nell'elegiaca meditazione, consiste
forse il nucleo da cui si sprigiona, nel suo concreto realizzarsi, la forza lirica del
Petrarca.*

This is surely true of the *Canzoniere* as a whole. The alternation between aesthetic contemplation and elegiac self-analysis continues throughout the collection. Neither stance can be assumed with more than temporary conviction, and yet any equilibrium between the two is hopelessly fragile. Perhaps this is why one's overall impression of the *Canzoniere* is so hard to reconcile with what appears to be its narrative intention. Seen in terms of its surface structure, the *Canzoniere* might seem to recount the journey of a soul towards salvation. From admiration of Laura's earthly beauty the poet passes to contemplation of her spiritual perfection in heaven, and this, in turn, gives way to the contemplation of God himself, a divine love which involves the renunciation of all vain human affections. It may well be that Petrarch had in mind the example of his beloved Saint Augustine with whom he debates so passionately in the *Secretum*, and there can be no doubt that after 1333 the poet meditated constantly on the *Confessions*. And yet, despite the Augustinian echoes that scholars have been at pains to document, the parallel between the *Confessions* and the *Canzoniere* is more indicative of intention than of achievement. Whereas all the vicissitudes of the saint's autobiography serve to demonstrate a preordained and unremitting movement towards God, it is precisely this sense of movement and purpose that is lacking in the *Canzoniere*. The surface structure, indicated above, disintegrates when we look more closely at the sequence of poems. Instead of progress we find an obsessive repetition of attitudes and situations. Even the difference between the poems *in vita* and the poems *in morte*, between the earthly and the heavenly Laura, is eventually blurred. If on earth Laura is frequently transformed into something like a minor deity (XC, CLIX, CCXLVIII), in heaven she is constantly humanized as an ideal mistress turning back to console her lover (CCCII, CCCXLVI, CCCLXII). Laura's death, therefore, does not mark a stage in the poet's spiritual progress; the vision of Laura as a work of art remains essentially the same. Only the strategy needed to create the aesthetic vision has to change.

9

On earth Laura had to be raised above the flesh; in heaven she has to be something less than pure spirit.

In this context the final turning to God of sonnets I and CCCLXV does not present itself as the logical conclusion of a coherent development, but rather as yet another recurrent state of mind. The fact is that we have been here before in sonnets LXII and CCLXXIII (not translated in this selection). Petrarch's *conversio* has, in any case, little to do with spiritual illumination. It arises from a deep sense of failure rather than from any vision of a long-sought truth.

> But now I see too well how I became
> a tale for common gossip everywhere,
> so that I grow ashamed of what I am;
>
> and of my raving still the fruit is shame,
> and penitence, and last the knowledge clear
> that all the world loves is a passing dream.

The poet turns to God, not in love and adoration, but in weariness and self-disgust. There is nothing in the *Canzoniere* like the thrill of recognition that rings through Augustine's *Sero te amavi*. Unlike the saint, Petrarch does not see the *conversio* as making sense out of his life; it is, at best, a release from a life that has been senseless. If the poet, at some point, shared the Augustinian intention of revealing God's providential purpose in terms of a single human life, then the title *Rerum vulgarium fragmenta* may assume a deeper significance as the implicit admission of a failure.

The recognition of a lack of progress and purpose is closely connected with Petrarch's insistence on the passing of time. He seems to write with the calendar at his elbow, noting with the precision of a diarist the anniversaries of his first meeting with Laura (CXXII, CCCLXIV, and many poems not included in this selection). The awareness of time serves only to reveal more clearly his trapped, unchanging condition. It threatens the artist's vision and reproves the artist. Sonnet CXC is a particularly instructive example. In the octave the poet reconstructs the vision of Laura, admitting that he has "left every task to follow her." In the final tercet the awareness of time returns:

> And now the sun had noon within its reach;
> with tired eyes, not sated, I fell down
> into the stream, and she was gone from me.

Lost in contemplation, neglecting his real work, the poet is suddenly disturbed by the recognition that his life has passed from dawn to noon, from youth to middle age. With this recognition the vision is destroyed. As the poet falls into one of the streams mentioned in the third line of the sonnet, we realize that all the time he has been standing still. The contemplation of Laura is revealed as a serious impediment to spiritual progress.

It is to this sense of paralysis and to a chronic emotional instability that we must relate the frequent use of antitheses, particularly in the sonnets. The use of antitheses is, of course, one of the most obvious features of the Petrarchan manner, and it is certainly an aspect of Petrarch that appealed strongly to the sonneteers of the sixteenth century. Perhaps the very thoroughness of the subsequent development has dimmed the brightness of the original for us today. The more Petrarch resembles his imitators the less we like him. Even for an age that has overcome the Romantic distrust for the more ostentatious forms of poetic ingenuity, the Petrarchan antitheses can still seem a dangerously repetitive, if not gratuitous kind of ornamentation. If we are ever to distinguish Petrarch from his less inspired followers, we must learn to see how the use of antitheses belongs to the very essence of the *Canzoniere*. Here, above all, we should test the truth of the old adage that in a work of art form and content are one. Let us look briefly at one of the most widely imitated sonnets, *S'amor non è* (CXXXII).

> And if this be not love, what is it then?
> but if it is love, God, what can love be?

if good, why mortal bitterness to me?
if ill, why is it sweetness that torments?

If willingly I burn, why these laments?
if not my will, what use can weeping be?
O living death, delightful agony,
how can you do so much where none consents?

And if I do consent, wrongly I grieve.
By such cross winds my fragile bark is blown
I drift unsteered upon the open seas:

in wisdom light, with error so weighed down
that I myself know not the thing I crave,
and burn in winter, and in summer freeze.

Only CXXXIV has a more extensive list of antitheses, and it must be admitted that neither sonnet is typical of the *Canzoniere*, which rarely goes to such lengths. Yet it may be useful to take an extreme example. If we can appreciate the antitheses here, we should have little trouble elsewhere.

The first thing to be noted is the skill of Petrarch in preventing his antitheses from becoming monotonous. The questions, for example, shift from "what" to "why" and "how" (*che, onde, come*) as if the lover were uncertain which line of questioning to adopt. The self-interrogation of the first six lines is interrupted by the sudden apostrophe of line seven and by a question addressed to love itself. In the sestet question gives way to statement, and abstractions (love, will, etc.) are replaced by an image (the unsteered ship) that embodies the contrasts of the lover's condition. There is an artful confusion between the objective and the subjective, between the nature of love and the nature of the lover. The sestet demonstrates his failure to separate the two. How can he know what love is when he does not know his own mind? Emilio Bigi has pointed out that the Petrarchan use of antitheses involves "a movement of recomposition," a harmony achieved largely through the symmetry within which the contrasts are contained.[5] But surely this is to say no more than that Petrarch finds a highly ordered form to express an inner disorder. There is no real paradox here. The truth is that Petrarch's antitheses convey both disorder and paralysis: disorder through the irreconcilable terms of the contrast, paralysis through the rigidity of the syntax. In this way the antitheses create yet another kind of aesthetic stasis. The inner discord becomes a subject for contemplation, and the contraries produce no progression.

This discussion of the Petrarchan antitheses will, I hope, serve as a limited, but instructive example of the way Petrarch works. The English reader is, indeed, ill-prepared for the *Canzoniere* if he regards it simply as a major source-book for the Elizabethan sonneteers. The Petrarchan conventions that the Renaissance poets exploited so exhaustively could hardly have provoked such imitation if they had not once served as the expression of a complex and original lyric genius.

The range of the *Canzoniere* is, no doubt, narrow in theme, imagery, and diction. After the cosmic vistas of Dante, the little world of Petrarch can produce an almost claustrophobic reaction. And yet the Petrarchan manner, through its very limits, through its obsessive repetitions, does bring a new dimension into European poetry. For the first time we have a self-conscious and introverted artist longing to take refuge in his art, seeking in a dream of ideal beauty a peace and a self-forgetting that is ultimately impossible to maintain. Threatened by both time and eternity, flesh and spirit, the aesthetic stasis embodied in the vision of Laura remains the only cause and cure of Petrarch's sickness: "one hand alone pierces and makes me whole" (CLXIV). There is nothing wrong with reading the *Canzoniere* as love story or Christian confession, but it surely has a greater claim on our attention as the self-revelation of an artistic temperament.

[5] Emilio Bigi, *Dal Petrarca al Leopardi* (Milan and Naples, 1954), pp. 1–6.

TRANSLATOR'S PREFACE

The story of Petrarchan translation in England is strangely disappointing. To put it simply, no distinguished poet has seriously tried his hand at Petrarch since the time of Wyatt and Surrey. There have been, in fact, only two basic English approaches to the *Canzoniere*, corresponding roughly to the sixteenth and nineteenth centuries. The Tudor poets found in Petrarch a master of technique, a source to be plundered and assimilated rather than translated. The Victorians sentimentalized him as a medieval embodiment of Romantic melancholy, but left translation to literary ladies, versifying gentlemen, and officers of the Indian Army. In the present century one can admire the idiosyncratic Anglo-Irish prose versions of J. M. Synge and the more conventional felicities of Morris Bishop, but no adequate selection from the *Canzoniere* has remained in print. The time is surely ripe for a new attempt.

This is not the place for an essay on the theory of translation. Most practising translators are, like Dryden, conscious of steering "betwixt the two extremes of paraphrase and literal translation," but the terms are vague, and the precise nature of the compromise usually escapes definition. One can only point to a limited number of specific problems and especially to those that one has failed to resolve.

The first problem to confront any translator of Petrarch is that of rhyme. Since the structure and argument of the sonnet are so closely linked to rhyme-scheme, it follows that rhyme cannot be lightly abandoned. Nor can one modify the Petrarchan rhyme-scheme into something like a Shakespearean sonnet without destroying the asymmetrical balance of octave and sestet in the Italian form. My own approach is an attempt to convey the original rhyme-scheme without making rhyme my primary concern. In other words, I have tried to avoid the obvious pitfalls of rhyme-hunting by mixing full rhyme with half-rhyme, unstressed rhyme, and assonance, sometimes settling for the merest echo of consonant or vowel. Some *a posteriori* justification for this procedure may be sought in the fact that Italian rhyme, simply because it is so easy, does not have the same heavy ring as full rhyme in English.

More complex, and in the long run more decisive for the success or failure of Petrarchan translation, is the question of diction. Petrarch's vocabulary is limited and decorous, avoiding almost completely both the colloquial and the erudite. Whereas the translator of the *Divine Comedy* finds himself stretched on the rack of Dante's immense linguistic range, the translator of the *Canzoniere* is cramped by the straitjacket of a uniform diction. To remain faithful to Petrarch he must shun both literary archaism and ostentatious modernity. The result can only be a rather neutral and conservative diction which runs the risk of flatness unless it is redeemed by a constant and precise attention to details of syntax, rhythm, and imagery. Inherent in this problem is Petrarch's obsessive use of words like *dolce, angelico, bello, leggiadro,* and *pietoso.* Here one must resist the temptation to multiply synonyms. Through constant repetition, certain words come to function almost as key-signatures, dictating the emotional tone of the poem. The ideal solution is to find a set of simple English equivalents and stick to them throughout, relying on the cumulative effect of context to suggest appropriate overtones. This, of course, is not always possible. There are no corresponding English adjectives for *leggiadro* and *pietoso* with their wealth of associations. And what can one do with the endless punning on *Laura, l'aura,* and *lauro?* One can only translate the sense that seems most obviously required by the context.

Petrarch's rhythm is generally regarded as remarkably smooth. Often there seems to be a contrast between the harmony of the verse and the inner discord it is supposed to express. When, in *S'io avesse pensato* (CCXCIII), Petrarch laments the loss of the sweet file needed to "make the rough dark verses smooth and clear," one is reminded of Tennyson:

> But, for the unquiet heart and brain,
> A use in measured language lies;
> The sad mechanic exercise,
> Like dull narcotics, numbing pain.

But that is only half the truth. Petrarch's rhythmic effects, though rarely striking, are many and subtle. One of the more obvious examples occurs in CCXCII where, after seven lines beginning with unstressed syllables, an unusually heavy stress falls on the climactic *poca polvere*. In English one can take some comfort from the flexibility of the iambic pentameter which is the traditional metre of the English sonnet and the nearest thing we have to *endecasillabi*. As for reproducing the Italian metre, it may be possible to write rhymed eleven-syllable lines in English, but my own attempts to do so sounded hopelessly foreign.

In general terms, my approach to the *Canzoniere* has been characterized by a desire to avoid the sentimental, the melodramatic, and the factitiously striking. I have not used the surprising adjective where Petrarch prefers the conventional, or the specific noun where he chooses the generic. I have avoided making his images more concrete than they are or his metaphors more metaphysical. Inevitably, I present a twentieth-century idea of what Petrarch is: this need not be the same as a contemporary view of what poetry should be. The Petrarchan manner represents a well-defined episode in the history of European literary fashion. It may be reinterpreted, but it cannot really be modernized. If it holds any interest for us, it must be accepted on its own terms.

Finally, a few words about the selection. I have omitted all the political poems in order to concentrate on the central theme of Laura. Two canzoni, two madrigals, and a sestina have been included to give some idea of the variety of forms. Roughly proportionate representation has been given to *In vita* and *In morte*. Otherwise, my selection reflects a compromise between what I originally intended to translate and what has proved amenable to translation. Among the omissions that I regret is the celebrated *Passa la nave mia* (CLXXXIX). I returned to this poem half-a-dozen times, but it never looked like coming out successfully, partly because I could not clear my mind of Wyatt's magnificent version, "My galley charged with forgetfulness." Under these circumstances, it would be foolish to invite comparison. The choice of the Wyatt version as an epigraph (p. 18) to my own work should be seen as a simple gesture of homage towards a predecessor whom one cannot hope to emulate.

In making these translations I have tried to keep in mind those students of English and Comparative Literature who so often hear the phrase "Petrarchan conventions" and so rarely have a chance to look at the poet himself. I hope they will discover that there is more to Petrarch than the conventions. As for those who know and love their Petrarch in the original, they will understand why I plead: *spero trovar pietà, non che perdono.*

Note on the Text

I have used throughout the text of the *Canzoniere* edited by Ferdinando Neri in *Francesco Petrarca: Rime, Trionfi e poesie latine* (Milan and Naples, 1951). For the notes I have relied heavily on the commentary of Giosuè Carducci and Severino Ferrari in their edition of *Le Rime di Francesco Petrarca* (Florence, 1899).

For the convenience of readers I have followed the conventional division of the *Canzoniere* into two parts entitled *In vita di Madonna Laura* and *In morte di Madonna Laura*. It should be noted, however, that this tradition does not have the authority of Petrarch himself. It is based on a note interpolated by an unknown hand on page 49 of the Vatican MS. 3195.

17

My galy charged with forgetfulnes
Thorrough sharpe sees in wynter nyghtes doeth pas
Twene Rock and Rock; and eke myn ennemy, Alas,
That is my lorde, sterith with cruelnes;

And every owre a thought in redines,
As tho that deth were light in suche a case;
An endles wynd doeth tere the sayll a pase
Of forced sightes and trusty ferefulnes.

A rayn of teris, a clowde of derk disdain
Hath done the wered cordes great hinderaunce,
Wrethed with errour and eke with ignoraunce.

The starres be hid that led me to this pain;
Drowned is reason that should me confort,
And I remain dispering of the port.

SIR THOMAS WYATT

IN VITA DI
MADONNA LAURA

I

Voi ch'ascoltate in rime sparse il suono
di quei sospiri ond'io nudriva 'l core
in sul mio primo giovenile errore
quand'era in parte altr'uom da quel ch'i' sono;

del vario stile in ch'io piango e ragiono,
fra le vane speranze e 'l van dolore,
ove sia chi per prova intenda amore,
spero trovar pietà, non che perdono.

Ma ben veggio or sì come al popol tutto
favola fui gran tempo, onde sovente
di me medesmo meco mi vergogno;

e del mio vaneggiar vergogna è 'l frutto
e 'l pentersi e 'l conoscer chiaramente
che quanto piace al mondo è breve sogno.

I

All you that hear in scattered rhymes the sound
of sighs on which I used to feed my heart
in my first youthful error when, in part,
I was another man, now left behind;

for the vain hopes, vain sorrows of my mind,
the tears and discourse of my varied art,
in any who have played a lover's part
pardon and pity too I hope to find.

But now I see too well how I became
a tale for common gossip everywhere,
so that I grow ashamed of what I am;

and of my raving still the fruit is shame
and penitence, and last the knowledge clear
that all the world loves is a passing dream.

III

Era il giorno ch'al sol si scolararo
per la pietà del suo fattore i rai;
quando i' fui preso, e non me ne guardai,
che i be' vostr'occhi, Donna, mi legaro.

Tempo non mi parea da far riparo
contr'a' colpi d'Amor; però m'andai
secur, senza sospetto; onde i miei guai
nel comune dolor s'incominciaro.

Trovommi Amor del tutto disarmato,
et aperta la via per gli occhi al core,
che di lagrime son fatti uscio e varco.

Però, al mio parer, non li fu onore
ferir me de saetta in quello stato,
a voi armata non mostrar pur l'arco.

III

It was that very day on which the sun
in awe of his creator dimmed the ray,
when I was captured, with my guard astray,
for your fine eyes, my lady, bound me then.

It hardly seemed the time for me to plan
defence against Love's stroke; I went my way
secure, unwary; so upon that day
of general sorrow all my pains began.

Love found me with no armour for the fight,
my eyes an open highway to the heart,
eyes that are now a vent for tears to flow.

And yet he played no honourable part,
wounding me with his shaft in such a state;
he saw you armed and dared not lift the bow.

XIII

Quando fra l'altre donne ad ora ad ora
Amor vien nel bel viso di costei,
quanto ciascuna è men bella di lei
tanto cresce 'l desio che m'innamora.

I' benedico il loco e 'l tempo e l'ora
che sì alto miraron gli occhi mei,
e dico: Anima, assai ringraziar dei,
che fosti a tanto onor degnata allora;

da lei ti ven l'amoroso pensero,
che mentre 'l segui al sommo ben t'invia,
poco prezzando quel ch'ogni uom desia;

da lei vien l'animosa leggiadria
ch'al ciel ti scorge per destro sentero:
sì ch'i' vo già de la speranza altero.

XIII

When sometimes Love is borne in her sweet face
and comes among the other ladies there,
as each one suddenly seems much less fair,
by so much does my will to love increase.

I bless the time, the very hour, the place,
that raised my eyes up to a height so rare,
and say: my soul, your thankfulness declare
that you were rendered worthy of such grace.

From her there comes to you the thought of love
which, if you follow, leads to highest good,
careless of all that other men regard;

from her there comes the blithe and graceful mood
that shows the fittest path to heaven above:
and thus my hope already seems to thrive.

XVI

Movesi il vecchierel canuto e bianco
del dolce loco ov'à sua età fornita
e da la famigliuola sbigottita
che vede il caro padre venir manco;

indi traendo poi l'antico fianco
per l'estreme giornate di sua vita
quanto più po col buon voler s'aita,
rotto dagli anni e dal cammino stanco;

e viene a Roma, seguendo 'l desio,
per mirar la sembianza di colui
ch'ancor lassù nel ciel vedere spera:

così, lasso, talor vo cercand'io,
Donna, quanto è possibile in altrui
la disiata vostra forma vera.

XVI

He moves, a pale and hoary-haired old man,
from his sweet home where years have passed away,
and from the little family in dismay
to think that now their father will be gone;

then, forcing stiffened shanks to stir again
through these last stages of his closing day,
he helps with his good will as best he may,
broken with age, and by the road undone;

and, urged by his desire, comes to Rome
to contemplate that image of the one
he hopes to see again in heaven above:

so I, alas, my lady, sometimes roam
to seek in other faces you alone,
some image of the one true form I love.

XXI

Mille fiate, o dolce mia guerrera,
per aver co' begli occhi vostri pace
v'aggio proferto il cor, m'a voi non piace
mirar sì basso colla mente altera;

e se di lui fors'altra donna spera,
vive in speranza debile e fallace:
mio, perché sdegno ciò ch'a voi dispiace,
esser non può già mai così com'era.

Or s'io lo scaccio, et e' non trova in voi
ne l'esilio infelice alcun soccorso,
né sa star sol, né gire ov'altri il chiama,

poria smarrire il suo natural corso:
che grave colpa fia d'ambeduo noi,
e tanto più de voi, quanto più v'ama.

XXI

A thousand times, O gentle warrior mine,
that I might peace with those fair eyes obtain
my heart I've offered, but you do not deign
to look so far below with haughty mind;

and if some other lady should incline
to hope in him, her hope is weak and vain:
since all that you reject I must disdain,
I shun the heart that can no more be mine.

Now if I chase him out, and he can find
no help from you upon his exiled way,
nor live alone, nor go where others care,

then from his nature's course the heart might stray:
so in us both the guilt would be profound,
but more in you because he loves you more.

XXII

A qualunque animale alberga in terra,
se non se alquanti ch'ànno in odio il sole,
tempo da travagliare è quanto è 'l giorno;
ma poi che 'l ciel accende le sue stelle
qual torna a casa e qual s'annida in selva   5
per aver posa almeno infin a l'alba.

Et io, da che comincia la bella alba
a scuoter l'ombra intorno de la terra,
svegliando gli animali in ogni selva,
non ò mai triegua di sospir col sole;   10
pur quand'io veggio fiammeggiar le stelle,
vo lagrimando e disiando il giorno.

Quando la sera scaccia il chiaro giorno,
e le tenebre nostre altrui fanno alba,
miro pensoso le crudeli stelle   15
che m'ànno fatto di sensibil terra,
e maledico il dì ch'i' vidi 'l sole;
che mi fa in vista un uom nudrito in selva.

Non credo che pascesse mai per selva
sì aspra fera, o di notte o di giorno,   20
come costei ch'i' piango a l'ombra e al sole,
e non mi stanca primo sonno od alba,
ché ben ch'i' sia mortal corpo di terra
lo mio fermo desir vien da le stelle.

Prima ch'i' torni a voi, lucenti stelle,   25
o tomi giù ne l'amorosa selva
lassando il corpo che fia trita terra,
vedess'io in lei pietà, che 'n un sol giorno
può ristorar molt'anni, e 'nanzi l'alba
puommi arricchir dal tramontar del sole.   30

XXII

For every animal that dwells on earth,
except for creatures that detest the sun,
the time of toil lasts only with the day;
but when the heaven kindles all its stars
they turn to home or nestle in the wood
to rest at least until the coming dawn.

And I, from that first hour when the dawn
scatters the darkness that surrounds the earth,
waking the animals in every wood,
can find no truce from sighs beneath the sun;
yet when I see the flaming of the stars,
I go about in tears and long for day.

When evening vanquishes the limpid day,
and what is shadow here elsewhere is dawn,
pensive I gaze upon the cruel stars
that framed my being of such feeling earth,
and curse the day I ever saw the sun;
so that I seem a wild man of the wood.

I do not think that ever in the wood
so fierce a creature grazed by night or day
as she that makes me weep in shade or sun,
not ceasing for the dusk or for the dawn,
for though my mortal body is of earth,
my fixed desire comes only from the stars.

Before I reascend to you, bright stars,
or fall below into the lovers' wood,
letting my body turn to crumbling earth,
could I but see her pity me, one day
would many years redeem, and until dawn
joy would enrich me from the setting sun.

Con lei foss'io da che si parte il sole
e non ci vedess'altri che le stelle,
sol una notte, e mai non fosse l'alba!
e non se transformasse in verde selva
per uscirmi di braccia, come il giorno
ch'Apollo la seguia qua giù per terra.

Ma io sarò sotterra in secca selva,
e 'l giorno andrà pien di minute stelle
prima ch'a sì dolce alba arrivi il sole.

Could I be with her where we lose the sun,
where none could spy on us except the stars,
one single endless night without a dawn!
nor she transform herself in verdant wood,
escaping from these arms, as on the day
Apollo once pursued her here on earth.

But I shall be in earth, closed in dry wood,
and day shall come studded with countless stars,
before so sweet a dawn beholds the sun.

XXXIV

Apollo, s'ancor vive il bel desio
che t'infiammava a le tesaliche onde,
e se non ài l'amate chiome bionde,
volgendo gli anni, già poste in oblio;

dal pigro gelo e dal tempo aspro e rio,
che dura quanto 'l tuo viso s'asconde,
difendi or l'onorata e sacra fronde
ove tu prima e poi fu' invescato io;

e per vertù de l'amorosa speme
che ti sostenne ne la vita acerba,
di queste impression l'aere disgombra.

Sì vedrem poi per meraviglia inseme
sedere la Donna nostra sopra l'erba
e far de le sue braccia a sé stessa ombra.

XXXIV

Apollo, should the fair desire still last
that burned you where Thessalian waters flow,
if golden tresses loved so long ago
be not forgotten with the ages past;

from biting weather and from sluggish frost
that stays as long as you conceal your brow,
protect the honoured and the sacred bough
where you were first ensnared and I am lost;

and still by virtue of the hope that then
sustained your love throughout the bitter life,
dispel the noxious vapours that pervade.

So shall we both marvel to see again
our lady sit upon the grassy turf
and make with her own arms her own sweet shade.

XXXV

Solo e pensoso i più deserti campi
vo mesurando a passi tardi e lenti,
e gli occhi porto per fuggire intenti
ove vestigio uman la rena stampi.

Altro schermo non trovo che mi scampi
dal manifesto accorger de le genti,
perché negli atti d'allegrezza spenti
di fuor si legge com'io dentro avvampi;

sì ch'io mi credo omai che monti e piagge
e fiumi e selve sappian di che tempre
sia la mia vita ch'è celata altrui.

Ma pur sì aspre vie né sì selvagge
cercar non so, ch'Amor non venga sempre
ragionando con meco, et io con lui.

XXXV

Alone in thought, the most deserted fields
I measure with a slow and halting pace,
with eyes intent to flee from any trace
of human presence in the sand revealed.

For my defence I find no other shield
against the people's open knowing gaze,
for in my bearing, empty of all joys,
they read the flame that burns in me concealed;

so that I think the mountain and the slope,
the wood and stream already understand
the temper of my life, to others dim.

And yet I cannot find a path so steep,
a way so wild that Love does not ascend,
discoursing with me still, and I with him.

XLIX

Perch'io t'abbia guardato di menzogna
a mio podere et onorato assai,
ingrata lingua, già però non m'ài
renduto onor, ma fatto ira e vergogna;

ché quanto più 'l tuo aiuto mi bisogna
per dimandar mercede, allor ti stai
sempre più fredda, e se parole fai
son imperfette e quasi d'uom che sogna.

Lagrime triste, e voi tutte le notti
m'accompagnate ov'io vorrei star solo,
poi fuggite dinanzi a la mia pace;

e voi, sì pronti a darmi angoscia e duolo,
sospiri, allor traete lenti e rotti;
solo la vista mia del cor non tace.

XLIX

Though from all lies I have preserved your fame,
giving you all the honour that I may,
ungrateful tongue, you do not yet repay
my faith with honour, but with wrath and shame;

for when I need you most to help my aim
in pleading for compassion, then you stay
more cold than ever, and what words you say
have the imperfect utterance of a dream.

And you, my sorrowing tears, each night you go
along with me when I would be alone,
and when my peace is near, then you depart;

and you, so prompt to give me grief and pain,
sighs, then you come so brokenly and slow:
my looks alone fail not to speak the heart.

LII

Non al suo amante più Diana piacque
quando per tal ventura tutta ignuda
la vide in mezzo de le gelide acque,

ch'a me la pastorella alpestra e cruda
posta a bagnar un leggiadretto velo,
ch'a l'aura il vago e biondo capel chiuda;

tal che mi fece, or quand'egli arde 'l cielo,
tutto tremar d'un amoroso gielo.

LII

The pleasure of Actaeon was no greater
when chance revealed in all her nakedness
Diana bathing in the icy water,

than mine at the raw mountain shepherdess
washing the airy veil she binds to save
her golden tresses from the wind's distress;

so, even now, when heaven burns above,
it makes me shiver in a frost of love.

LXXIV

Io son già stanco di pensar sì come
i miei pensier in voi stanchi non sono,
e come vita ancor non abbandono
per fuggir de' sospir sì gravi some;

e come a dir del viso e de le chiome
e de' begli occhi ond'io sempre ragiono
non è mancata omai la lingua e 'l suono,
dì e notte chiamando il vostro nome;

e che' piè miei non son fiaccati e lassi
a seguir l'orme vostre in ogni parte
perdendo inutilmente tanti passi;

et onde vien l'enchiostro, onde le carte
ch'i vo empiendo di voi; se 'n ciò fallassi,
colpa d'Amor, non già defetto d'arte.

LXXIV

I am already weary of the thought
of how my thought in you unwearied lies,
and how, to flee the burden of my sighs,
my heavy life has still not taken flight;

and how, in speaking of the face so bright,
ever discoursing of the hair and eyes,
there lacks not yet the tongue, the voice that cries,
calling upon your name by day and night;

and how my feet untiringly travail
in following your traces everywhere,
wasting so many steps to no avail;

and whence comes ink and paper which I dare
to fill with you; if doing so I fail,
Love is to blame, no fault of art is there.

XC

Erano i capei d'oro a l'aura sparsi
che 'n mille dolci nodi gli avolgea,
e 'l vago lume oltra misura ardea
di quei begli occhi ch'or ne son sì scarsi;

e 'l viso di pietosi color farsi,
non so se vero o falso, mi parea:
i' che l'esca amorosa al petto avea,
qual meraviglia se di subito arsi?

Non era l'andar suo cosa mortale
ma d'angelica forma, e le parole
sonavan altro che pur voce umana;

uno spirto celeste, un vivo sole
fu quel ch'i' vidi, e se non fosse or tale,
piaga per allentar d'arco non sana.

XC

Upon the breeze she spread her golden hair
that in a thousand gentle knots was turned,
and the sweet light beyond all measure burned
in eyes where now that radiance is rare;

and in her face there seemed to come an air
of pity, true or false, that I discerned:
I had love's tinder in my breast unburned,
was it a wonder if it kindled there?

She moved not like a mortal, but as though
she bore an angel's form, her words had then
a sound that simple human voices lack;

a heavenly spirit, a living sun
was what I saw; now, if it is not so,
the wound's not healed because the bow grows slack.

CVI

Nova angeletta sovra l'ale accorta
scese dal cielo in su la fresca riva
là 'nd'io passava sol per mio destino.

Poi che senza compagna e senza scorta
mi vide, un laccio che di seta ordiva
tese fra l'erba ond'è verde il camino.

Allor fui preso, e non mi spiacque poi,
sì dolce lume uscìa degli occhi suoi!

CVI

A wondrous angel came down from the sky
on nimble wings to that cool river where
it was my destiny to walk alone.

Without a friend or guide I wandered by,
and, seeing this, she laid a silken snare
amid the grass that made the pathway green.

Then was I caught, and after had no care,
her eyes were shining with a light so fair.

CXXII

Dicessette anni à già rivolto il cielo
poi che 'mprima arsi, e già mai non mi spensi,
ma quando avèn ch'al mio stato ripensi
sento nel mezzo de le fiamme un gelo.

Vero è 'l proverbio, ch'altri cangia il pelo
anzi che 'l vezzo, e per lentar i sensi
gli umani affetti non son meno intensi;
ciò ne fa l'ombra ria del grave velo.

Oi me lasso! e quando fia quel giorno
che mirando il fuggir de gli anni miei
esca del foco e di sì lunghe pene?

Vedrò mai il dì che pur quant'io vorrei
quell'aria dolce del bel viso adorno
piaccia a quest'occhi, e quanto si convene?

CXXII

The sky has turned through seventeen years since first
I burned with fire that is never spent,
yet when I think upon my state I sense
even amid the flames a touch of frost.

The fur may change, the vice will not be lost,
says a true proverb; failing of the sense
makes not the human passions less intense;
such is the shade our heavy veil has cast.

Alas, and shall I ever see the day
when, contemplating all my years in flight,
I shun the fire and this long misery?

Shall the day come when, with no more delight
than I could wish, that face's beauty may
gladden my eyes, and to a just degree?

CXXVI

Chiare fresche e dolci acque
ove le belle membra
pose colei che sola a me par donna;
gentil ramo ove piacque,
con sospir mi rimembra,   5
a lei di fare al bel fianco colonna;
erba e fior che la gonna
leggiadra ricoverse
co l'angelico seno;
aere sacro sereno   10
ove Amor co' begli occhi il cor m'aperse:
date udienzia insieme
a le dolenti mie parole estreme.

S'egli è pur mio destino,
e 'l cielo in ciò s'adopra,   15
ch'Amor quest'occhi lagrimando chiuda,
qualche grazia il meschino
corpo fra voi ricopra
e torni l'alma al proprio albergo ignuda;
la morte fia men cruda   20
se questa spene porto
a quel dubbioso passo,
ché lo spirito lasso
non poria mai in più riposato porto
né in più tranquilla fossa   25
fuggir la carne travagliata e l'ossa.

CXXVI

Waters fresh and sweet and clear
where the fair limbs reclined
of the one creature who to me seems woman;
and gentle tree-trunk where,
with sighs I call to mind,
the leaning side once loved to find a column;
flowers and grass that often
the light gown hid from sight
with the angelic breast;
airs breathing holy rest
where Love with those fair eyes opened my heart:
come, and together grant
a hearing to my last lament.

If it be destiny,
and heaven works for this,
that Love should close these weeping eyes of mine,
then may some kindness lay
the body in your midst
and the soul naked to its home return;
death shall become less stern
if such a hope I bear
into that fearful pass,
for the soul's weariness
could find no calmer haven anywhere,
nor could it ever leave
the troubled flesh in a more quiet grave.

Tempo verrà ancor forse
ch'a l'usato soggiorno
torni la fera bella e mansueta
a là 'v'ella mi scorse   30
nel benedetto giorno
volga la vista disiosa e lieta,
cercandomi; ed o pieta!
già terra infra le pietre
vedendo, Amor l'ispiri   35
in guisa che sospiri
sì dolcemente che mercé m'impetre,
e faccia forza al cielo
asciugandosi gli occhi col bel velo.

Da' be' rami scendea,   40
dolce ne la memoria,
una pioggia di fior sovra 'l suo grembo,
ed ella si sedea
umile in tanta gloria,
coverta già de l'amoroso nembo;   45
qual fior cadea sul lembo,
qual su le treccie bionde,
ch'oro forbito e perle
eran quel dì a vederle;
qual si posava in terra e qual su l'onde,   50
qual con un vago errore
girando parea dir: "Qui regna Amore".

A time may come again
when she perhaps will stray
to the old haunt, untamed, yet fair and meek,
and where she saw me then
upon that blessed day
will turn an eager and a happy look,
and there, O pity! seek
and find me turned to dust amid the stones:
at this may Love arise,
inspiring her with sighs
so sweet she forces heaven and obtains
its mercy for my soul,
drying her eyes upon the lovely veil.

From the fair boughs there fell,
sweet in the memory,
upon her lap a rain of every flower,
and she sat there and still
was humble in such glory,
already covered by the loving shower;
upon the hem lay flowers,
and some the tresses crowned
which seemed that day to hold
both pearls and polished gold;
some rested on the waves, some on the ground;
some, sweetly turning through the air,
seemed in their drift to whisper: "Love reigns here."

Quante volte diss'io
allor pien di spavento:
"Costei per fermo nacque in paradiso!"   55
Così carco d'oblio
il divin portamento
e 'l volto e le parole e 'l dolce riso
m'aveano, e sì diviso
da l'imagine vera,   60
ch'i' dicea sospirando:
"Qui come venn'io o quando?"
credendo esser in ciel, non là dov'era.
Da indi in qua mi piace
quest'erba sì ch'altrove non ò pace.   65

Se tu avessi ornamenti quant'ài voglia,
poresti arditamente
uscir del bosco e gir infra la gente.

How often I exclaimed,
seized by a sudden fear:
"For certain she was born in Paradise!"
Such deep oblivion came
from her celestial air,
the words, the gentle smiling, and the eyes,
so faintly did I seize
the image truth would show,
that I said sighing then:
"How came I here, or when?"
thinking myself in heaven, not here below.
And ever since I've loved this place
so much that elsewhere I can find no peace.

Song, had you beauty as you have desire,
intrepidly you could
go out among the crowd and leave this wood.

CXXIX

Di pensier in pensier, di monte in monte
mi guida Amor, ch'ogni segnato calle
provo contrario a la tranquilla vita.
Se 'n solitaria piaggia, rivo o fonte,
se 'nfra duo poggi siede ombrosa valle,   5
ivi s'acqueta l'alma sbigottita;
e come Amor l'envita
or ride or piange, or teme or s'assecura;
e 'l volto che lei segue ov'ella il mena
si turba e rasserena,   10
et in un esser picciol tempo dura;
onde a la vista uom di tal vita esperto
diria: "Questo arde, e di suo stato è incerto".

Per alti monti e per selve aspre trovo
qualche riposo: ogni abitato loco   15
è nemico mortal de gli occhi miei.
A ciascun passo nasce un penser novo
de la mia donna, che sovente in gioco
gira 'l tormento ch'i' porto per lei;
et a pena vorrei   20
cangiar questo mio viver dolce amaro
ch'i' dico: "Forse ancor ti serva Amore
ad un tempo migliore;
forse a te stesso vile, altrui se' caro";
et in questa trapasso sospirando: 25
"Or porebbe esser vero? or come? or quando?"

CXXIX

From thought to thought, from mountainside to mountain
Love leads me on, since every beaten trail
I feel as hostile to my peace of mind.
If some deserted heath has stream or fountain,
or if two hills should hide a shadowed vale,
the spirit sees its suffering decline,
and there, as Love designs,
now laughs and weeps, now fears and learns to trust;
the face that follows where the spirit leads
grows clear and overclouds,
and no condition ever seems to last:
so, at the sight, a man who knew that life
would say: "He burns, and stands in doubtful strife."

Among high mountains and wild woods I find
some kind of rest; but each frequented place
becomes an enemy that my eyes abhor.
At every step a new thought comes to mind
of my dear lady, often bringing gladness
out of the torment that I feel for her;
and hardly would I prefer
to change the sweet and bitter life I bear
when I reflect: "Perhaps Love keeps in view
a better time for you;
you hate yourself, but she may hold you dear."
And with this thought sighing I change again:
"Can it be ever true? but how? and when?"

Ove porge ombra un pino alto od un colle,
talor m'arresto, e pur nel primo sasso
disegno co la mente il suo bel viso.
Poi ch'a me torno trovo il petto molle   30
de la pietate, et allor dico: "Ahi lasso,
dove se' giunto, et onde se' diviso!"
Ma mentre tener fiso
posso al primo pensier la mente vaga,
e mirar lei et obliar me stesso,   35
sento Amor sì da presso
che del suo proprio error l'alma s'appaga:
in tante parti e sì bella la veggio,
che se l'error durasse altro non cheggio.

I' l'ò più volte, or chi fia che m'il creda?   40
ne l'acqua chiara e sopra l'erba verde
veduto viva, e nel troncon d'un faggio,
e 'n bianca nube, sì fatta che Leda
avria ben detto che sua figlia perde
come stella che 'l sol copre col raggio;   45
e quanto in più selvaggio
loco mi trovo e 'n più deserto lido,
tanto più bella il mio pensier l'adombra.
Poi quando il vero sgombra
quel dolce error, pur lì medesmo assido   50
me freddo, pietra morta in pietra viva,
in guisa d'uom che pensi e pianga e scriva.

Where a tall pine-tree or a hill gives shade
sometimes I stop, and on the nearest stone
my mind will draw her face. At last I find,
on coming to myself, my breast is bathed
with that emotion; then "alas," I groan,
"where are you now? what have you left behind?"
But while my wandering mind
can be kept steadfastly on that first thought
and I forget myself and gaze on her,
then I feel Love so near
the soul is sated with its own deceit:
I see her in so many things, so fair,
that if the illusion lasts I ask no more.

Often I've seen (who will believe me now?)
on the green grass or in transparent water
her living self, in beech-trees or the face
of a white cloud, and ever fashioned so
that Leda would have surely said her daughter
fades like a star outshone by the sun's rays;
and the more wild the place
I come upon, the lonelier the shore,
the fairer does thought shadow forth my love.
Then, when the truth removes
that sweet illusion, I sit as before,
cold and stone-dead upon the living stone,
like one who thinks and weeps and writes alone.

Ove d'altra montagna ombra non tocchi
verso 'l maggiore e 'l più espedito giogo,
tirar mi suol un desiderio intenso.   55
Indi i miei danni a misurar con gli occhi
comincio e 'ntanto lagrimando sfogo
di dolorosa nebbia il cor condenso,
allor ch'i' miro e penso
quanta aria dal bel viso mi diparte,   60
che sempre m'è sì presso e sì lontano;
poscia fra me pian piano:
"Che sai tu, lasso? forse in quella parte
or di tua lontananza si sospira";
et in questo penser l'alma respira.   65

Canzone, oltra quell'alpe,
là dove il ciel è più sereno e lieto,
mi rivedrai sovr'un ruscel corrente
ove l'aura si sente
d'un fresco et odorifero laureto: 70
ivi è 'l mio cor, e quella che 'l m'invola;
qui veder pòi l'imagine mia sola.

To where the mountain shadows never lie,
towards the highest and best vantage-point,
a fierce desire often makes me start.
There I begin to measure with the eye
my sufferings, and tearfully give vent
to the sad mists that thicken in my heart,
when both my gaze and thought
span all that lies between me and the fair
face that is still so near and far away;
then, whispering to myself, I say:
"What can you know? this moment over there
perhaps your absence makes her sigh for you;"
and in this thought the spirit breathes anew.

My song, beyond this alp,
where skies are happier and clear above,
you'll find me sitting by a stream that flows
where gentle aura blows
in from a fresh and fragrant laurel-grove:
there is my heart and she that stole it from me;
and here my image all that you can see.

CXXXII

S'amor non è, che dunque è quel ch'io sento?
ma s'egli è amor, per Dio, che cosa e quale?
so bona, ond'è l'effetto aspro mortale?
se ria, ond'è sì dolce ogni tormento?

S'a mia voglia ardo, ond'è 'l pianto e lamento?
s'a mal mio grado, il lamentar che vale?
O viva morte, o dilettoso male,
come puoi tanto in me, s'io nol consento?

E s'io 'l consento, a gran torto mi doglio.
Fra sì contrari venti in frale barca
mi trovo in alto mar senza governo:

sì lieve di saver, d'error sì carca,
ch'i' medesmo non so quel ch'io mi voglio,
e tremo a mezza state, ardendo il verno.

CXXXII

And if this be not love, what is it then?
but if it is love, God, what can love be?
if good, why mortal bitterness to me?
if ill, why is it sweetness that torments?

If willingly I burn, why these laments?
if not my will, what use can weeping be?
O living death, delightful agony,
how can you do so much where none consents?

And if I do consent, wrongly I grieve.
But such cross winds my fragile bark is blown
I drift unsteered upon the open seas:

in wisdom light, with error so weighed down
that I myself know not the thing I crave,
and burn in winter, and in summer freeze.

CXXXIV

Pace non trovo e non ò da far guerra,
e temo e spero, et ardo e son un ghiaccio,
e volo sopra 'l cielo e giaccio in terra,
e nulla stringo e tutto 'l mondo abbraccio.

Tal m'à in pregion, che non m'apre né serra,
né per suo mi riten né scioglie il laccio,
e non m'ancide Amore e non mi sferra,
né mi vuol vivo né mi trae d'impaccio.

Veggio senza occhi e non ò lingua e grido,
e bramo di perir e cheggio aita,
et ò in odio me stesso ed amo altrui.

Pascomi di dolor, piangendo rido,
egualemente mi spiace morte e vita:
in questo stato son, Donna, per vui.

CXXXIV

I find no peace, and have no arms for war,
and fear and hope, and burn and yet I freeze,
and fly to heaven, lying on earth's floor,
and nothing hold, and all the world I seize.

My jailer opens not, nor locks the door,
nor binds me to her, nor will loose my ties;
Love kills me not, nor breaks the chains I wear,
nor wants me living, nor will grant me ease.

I have no tongue, and shout; eyeless, I see;
I long to perish, and I beg for aid;
I love another, and myself I hate.

Weeping I laugh, I feed on misery,
by death and life so equally dismayed:
for you, my lady, am I in this state.

CXL

Amor, che nel penser mio vive e regna
e 'l suo seggio maggior nel mio cor tene,
talor armato ne la fronte vene;
ivi si loca et ivi pon sua insegna.

Quella ch'amare e sofferir ne 'nsegna,
e vol che 'l gran desio, l'accesa spene,
ragion, vergogna, e reverenza affrene,
di nostro ardir fra se stessa si sdegna.

Onde Amor paventoso fugge al core,
lasciando ogni sua impresa, e piange e trema;
ivi s'asconde e non appar più fore.

Che poss'io far, temendo il mio signore,
se non star seco infin a l'ora estrema?
ché bel fin fa chi ben amando more.

CXL

Love, who within my thought still lives and reigns
and in my heart keeps his chief residence,
sometimes into my brow makes armed advance,
to plant his banner and his camp maintain.

Then she who teaches us both love and pain,
and wills that burning hope, desire intense,
be checked by reason, shame, and reverence,
receives our ardour with a deep disdain.

So fearful Love turns to the heart in flight,
leaving his enterprise, to weep and cower;
and there he hides and dare not venture out.

What can I do, seeing my master's fright,
except stay with him to the final hour?
His death is fair whose love is in the right.

CLIX

In qual parte del ciel, in quale idea
era l'esempio onde natura tolse
quel bel viso leggiadro, in ch'ella volse
mostrar qua giù quanto lassù potea?

Qual ninfa in fonti, in selve mai qual dea
chiome d'oro sì fino a l'aura sciolse?
quando un cor tante in sé vertuti accolse?
benché la somma è di mia morte rea.

Per divina bellezza indarno mira,
chi gli occhi de costei già mai non vide,
come soavemente ella gli gira;

non sa come Amor sana e come ancide
chi non sa come dolce ella sospira
e come dolce parla e dolce ride.

CLIX

What part of heaven, what idea gave
the perfect model in which Nature found
that glad and lovely face where she designed
to show below all she could do above?

What nymph in fountain, goddess in the grove,
could loose such fine gold hair upon the wind?
when did one heart so many virtues bound?
although the sum will lead me to the grave.

He seeks in vain where heavenly beauty lies
who has not seen my lady and has still
not marked the gentle glancing of her eyes;

he knows not how Love heals and how he kills
who knows not all the sweetness of her sighs
and how she sweetly speaks and sweetly smiles.

CLXIV

Or che 'l ciel e la terra e 'l vento tace,
e le fere e gli augelli il sonno affrena,
notte il carro stellato in giro mena
e nel suo letto il mar senz'onda giace;

vegghio, penso, ardo, piango, e chi mi sface
sempre m'è inanzi per mia dolce pena;
guerra è 'l mio stato, d'ira e di duol piena,
e sol di lei pensando ò qualche pace.

Così sol d'una chiara fonte viva
move 'l dolce e l'amaro ond'io mi pasco;
una man sola mi risana e punge;

e perché 'l mio martir non giunga a riva,
mille volte il dì moro e mille nasco:
tanto da la salute mia son lunge!

CLXIV

Now silence holds the wind and earth and skies,
and birds and beasts are checked by slumber's rein,
night leads upon its round the starry wain
and waveless in its bed the ocean lies;

I wake, think, burn, and weep, and still my eyes
see the destroyer who is my sweet pain;
war is my state where wrath and sorrow reign,
and only in the thought of her is peace.

So from one clear and living fountain pour
the sweet and bitter that I feed upon;
one hand alone pierces and makes me whole;

and that my martyrdom should reach no shore,
a thousand lives each day I lose and gain:
so far from all salvation is my soul!

CLXIX

Pien d'un vago penser che me desvia
da tutti gli altri e fammi al mondo ir solo,
ad or ad ora a me stesso m'involo,
pur lei cercando che fuggir devria,

e veggiola passar sì dolce e ria
che l'alma trema per levarsi a volo,
tal d'armàti sospir conduce stuolo
questa bella d'Amor nemica e mia!

Ben, s'i' non erro, di pietate un raggio
scorgo fra 'l nubiloso altero ciglio
che 'n parte rasserena il cor doglioso;

allor raccolgo l'alma, e poi ch'i' aggio
di scovrirle il mio mal preso consiglio
tanto gli ò a dir che 'ncominciar non oso.

CLXIX

Rapt in the one fond thought that makes me stray
from other men and walk this world alone,
sometimes I have escaped myself and flown
to seek the very one that I should flee;

so fair and fell I see her passing by
that the soul trembles to take flight again,
so many armèd sighs are in her train,
this lovely foe to Love himself and me!

And yet, upon that high and clouded brow
I seem to see a ray of pity shine,
shedding some light across the grieving heart:

so I call back my soul, and when I vow
at last to tell her of my hidden pain,
I have so much to say I dare not start.

CLXXX

Po, ben puo' tu portartene la scorza
di me con tue possenti e rapide onde;
ma lo spirto ch'iv'entro si nasconde
non cura né di tua né d'altrui forza:

lo qual, senz'alternar poggia con orza,
dritto per l'aure al suo desir seconde,
battendo l'ali verso l'aurea fronde,
l'acqua e 'l vento e la vela e i remi sforza.

Re degli altri, superbo, altero fiume,
ch'encontri 'l sol quando e' ne mena 'l giorno
e 'n ponente abbandoni un più bel lume,

tu te ne vai col mio mortal sul corno;
l'altro, coverto d'amorose piume,
torna volando al suo dolce soggiorno.

CLXXX

Po, on your powerful and rapid course,
you well may bear what is the husk of me;
the spirit that lies hidden there is free
from thought of you or any other force:

and, without tack to port or starboard, soars
through airs that help desire on its way,
winging towards the gold-branched laurel tree,
defying wind and water, sail and oars.

Proud, haughty river, king of all the rest,
you meet the sun when he conducts the dawn,
but leave a greater splendor in the west;

you bear my mortal body on your horn;
my better part, in loving plumage dressed,
rises towards its home in sweet return.

CLXXXI

Amor fra l'erbe una leggiadra rete
d'oro e di perle tese sott'un ramo
dell'arbor sempre verde ch'i' tant'amo,
benché n'abbia ombre più triste che liete.

L'esca fu 'l seme ch'egli sparge e miete,
dolce et acerbo, ch'i' pavento e bramo;
le note non fur mai, dal dì ch'Adamo
aperse gli occhi, sì soavi e quete;

e 'l chiaro lume che sparir fa 'l sole
folgorava dintorno, e 'l fune avolto
era a la man ch'avorio e neve avanza.

Così caddi a la rete; e qui m'àn colto
gli atti vaghi e l'angeliche parole
e 'l piacer e 'l desire e la speranza.

CLXXXI

Amid the grass Love delicately spread
a net of gold and pearls under a bough
of the dear evergreen I love, although
it holds more grief than gladness in its shade.

The bait he sowed and gathered was the seed,
bitter and sweet, my fear and longing now;
never were notes so gentle and so low
since the first day when Adam raised his head;

and the clear light, forcing the sun to hide,
flashed all about, and in a hand more white
than ivory or snow was wound the rope.

So in the net I fell; here was I caught
by the fair motions and angelic words,
the pleasure, the desire, and the hope.

CXC

Una candida cerva sopra l'erba
verde m'apparve, con duo corna d'oro,
fra due riviere, all'ombra d'un alloro,
levando 'l sole a la stagione acerba.

Era sua vista si dolce superba
ch'i' lasciai per seguirla ogni lavoro,
come l'avaro che 'n cercar tesoro
con diletto l'affanno disacerba.

"Nessun mi tocchi" al bel collo d'intorno
scritto avea di diamanti e di topazi,
"libera farmi al mio Cesare parve".

Et era 'l sol già volto al mezzo giorno;
gli occhi miei stanchi di mirar, non sazi,
quand'io caddi ne l'acqua, et ella sparve.

CXC

On the green grass a hind of candid white
appeared to me beneath a laurel's cover,
with golden horns, between two rivers,
in the unripe season and the dawning light.

There was such pride and sweetness in the sight
that I left every task to follow her,
like some old miser who, in seeking treasure,
consoles his bitter toil with that delight.

Around her neck there hung "let no-one touch"
in diamond and topaz written plain,
"it pleased my Caesar's will to make me free."

And now the sun had noon within its reach;
with tired eyes, not sated, I fell down
into the stream, and she was gone from me.

CXCII

Stiamo, Amor, a veder la gloria nostra,
cose sopra natura altere e nove.
Vedi ben quanta in lei dolcezza piove,
vedi lume che 'l cielo in terra mostra!

Vedi quant'arte dora e 'mperla e 'nostra
l'abito eletto e mai non visto altrove,
che dolcemente i piedi e gli occhi move
per questa di bei colli ombrosa chiostra!

L'erbetta verde e i fior di color mille
sparsi sotto quell'elce antiqua e negra,
pregan pur che 'l bel pè li prema o tocchi;

e 'l ciel di vaghe e lucide faville
s'accende intorno, e 'n vista si rallegra
d'esser fatto seren da sì belli occhi.

CXCII

Love, let us stay, our glory to behold,
things passing nature, wonderful and rare.
See how much sweetness rains upon her there,
see the pure light of heaven on earth revealed!

See how art decks with purple, pearls and gold
the chosen habit, never seen elsewhere,
giving the feet and eyes their motion fair
through this dark cloister that the hills enfold!

Blooms of a thousand colours, grasses green,
under the ancient blackened oak now pray
her foot may press or touch them where they rise;

and the sky, radiant with a glittering sheen,
kindles around, and visibly is gay
to be made cloudless by such lovely eyes.

CXCIX

O bella man che mi destringi 'l core
e 'n poco spazio la mia vita chiudi,
man ov'ogni arte e tutti loro studi
poser natura e 'l ciel per farsi onore;

di cinque perle oriental colore,
e sol ne le mie piaghe acerbi e crudi,
diti schietti soavi, a tempo ignudi,
consente or voi, per arrichirme, Amore.

Candido, leggiadretto e caro guanto,
che copria netto avorio e fresche rose,
chi vide mai al mondo sì dolci spoglie?

Così avess'io del bel velo altrettanto!
O inconstanzia de l'umane cose:
pur questo è furto, e vien ch'i' me ne spoglie.

CXCIX

You lovely hand that grip my heart so tight,
my life enclosing in a little space,
a hand in which both heaven and nature place
all study, every art, to show their might;

and those five pearls of orient colour bright,
that only in my wounds leave such sharp trace,
sweet slender fingers, now Love has the grace
to bare you for a while to my delight.

Spotless and delicate and dearest glove,
fresh roses and pure ivory encasing,
when had the world such gentle spoils to show?

If I could thus the lovely veil remove!
But O the transience of human things:
even this is theft, and I must let it go.

CCI

Mia ventura et Amor m'avean sì adorno
d'un bello aurato e serico trapunto,
ch'al sommo del mio ben quasi era aggiunto,
pensando meco: "A chi fu quest'intorno?"

Né mi riede a la mente mai quel giorno
che mi fe' ricco e povero in un punto,
ch'i' non sia d'ira e di dolor compunto,
pien di vergogna e d'amoroso scorno,

che la mia nobil preda non più stretta
tenni al bisogno, e non fui più costante
contra lo sforzo sol d'un'angioletta,

o, fuggendo, ale non giunsi a le piante
per far almen di quella man vendetta
che de li occhi mi trae lagrime tante.

CCI

Love and my lucky chance had granted me
such gold and silk embroidered loveliness
that I was almost at the height of bliss
as I reflected: "Think where once it lay!"

Now I can never call to mind the day
that made me rich, then left me poor no less,
without a stab of anger and distress,
a sense of shame and of love's mockery,

that I held not my noble prize more tight
when the need was, and made no firmer stand
against a little angel's meagre force;

or, fleeing, gave no wings unto my feet
to take at least some vengeance on the hand
that in these eyes provokes so many tears.

CCXXIV

S'una fede amorosa, un cor non finto,
un languir dolce, un desiar cortese;
s'oneste voglie in gentil foco accese,
un lungo error in cieco laberinto;

se ne la fronte ogni penser depinto
od in voci interotte a pena intese,
or da paura or da vergogna offese;
s'un pallor di viola e d'amor tinto;

s'aver altrui più caro che se stesso;
se sospirare e lagrimar mai sempre,
pascendosi di duol, d'ira e d'affanno;

s'arder da lunge et agghiacciar da presso
son le cagion ch'amando i' mi distempre:
vostro, Donna, 'l peccato, e mio fia 'l danno.

CCXXIV

If loving constancy, a heart unfeigned,
languishing sweet and courteous desire;
if honest will kindled in gentle fire,
long straying in a labyrinth that's blind;

if thoughts that in the brow depict the mind,
or broken words that one can hardly hear,
impeded now with shame and now with fear;
if pallor with love's violet combined;

if more than self to hold another dear;
if sighing still and weeping constantly,
feeding on care, on sorrow and disdain;

if burning from afar and freezing near,
are reasons why in love I thus decay,
yours, Lady, is the sin, and mine the pain.

CCXXXIV

O cameretta, che già fosti un porto
a le gravi tempeste mie diurne,
fonte se' or di lagrime notturne
che 'l dì celate per vergogna porto.

O letticciuol, che requie eri e conforto
in tanti affanni, di che dogliose urne
ti bagna Amor con quelle mani eburne,
solo ver me crudeli a sì gran torto.

Né pur il mio secreto e 'l mio riposo
fuggo, ma più me stesso e 'l mio pensero,
che, seguendol, talor levommi a volo;

e'l vulgo, a me nemico et odioso,
chi 'l pensò mai? per mio refugio chero:
tal paura ò di ritrovarmi solo.

CCXXXIV

O little room that used to be a port
after the raging tempests of the day,
now you provoke the nightly tears that I
daily for shame bear hidden in my thought.

O humble bed that rest and solace brought
in fretful cares, what urns of misery
Love pours upon you with those ivory
hands that of me alone make cruel sport.

Not only from my solitude and rest,
but from myself I flee and from the thought
that gave me once the wings on which I've flown;

and now the crowd, the foe that I detest,
(who would believe it?) is my last resort:
so much I fear to find myself alone.

CCXLV

Due rose fresche e colte in paradiso
l'altr'ier, nascendo il dì primo di maggio,
bel dono e d'un amante antiquo e saggio
tra duo minori egualmente diviso,

con sì dolce parlar e con un riso
da far innamorare un uom selvaggio,
di sfavillante ed amoroso raggio
e l'un' e l'altro fe' cangiare il viso.

"Non vede un simil par d'amanti il sole"
dicea ridendo e sospirando inseme;
e stringendo ambedue, volgeasi a torno.

Così partia le rose e le parole,
onde 'l cor lasso ancor s'allegra e teme:
o felice eloquenzia! o lieto giorno!

CCXLV

Two roses fresh and in some paradise
but newly culled on the first dawn of May,
a gift for two young lovers equally
divided by a lover old and wise,

who, with sweet words and with a smile to seize
a savage man and turn him to love's way,
brought forth a loving blush, a sparkling ray,
transforming both the faces where it rose.

"The sun sees not another pair like this"
with intermingled smiles and sighs he said;
and so, embracing both, he turned away.

So he bestowed roses and words on us;
they still revive my heart with hope and dread:
O happy eloquence! O joyful day!

CCXLVIII

Chi vuol veder quantunque po natura
e 'l ciel tra noi, venga a mirar costei,
ch'è sola un sol, non pur a li occhi mei,
ma al mondo cieco che vertù non cura;

e venga tosto, perché morte fura
prima i migliori e lascia star i rei;
questa, aspettata al regno delli dei,
cosa bella mortal passa e non dura.

Vedrà, s'arriva a tempo, ogni vertute,
ogni bellezza, ogni real costume
giunti in un corpo con mirabil tempre;

allor dirà che mie rime son mute,
l'ingegno offeso dal soverchio lume:
ma se più tarda avrà da pianger sempre.

CCXLVIII

If you would see what nature's hand can raise
and heaven on earth, come here and gaze on one
who not for me alone shines like the sun,
but for the blind world, careless where virtue lies;

and come in haste, for death too soon will seize
upon the best and led the bad remain:
so she, awaited in the gods' domain,
a lovely mortal thing, not long endures.

You will behold, if you arrive in time,
each virtue, beauty, royalty of mind
joined in one body to a wondrous temper;

then you will say that silent is my rhyme,
excess of light striking invention blind:
but more delay will make you weep for ever.

CCL

Solea lontana in sonno consolarme
con quella dolce angelica sua vista
madonna, or mi spaventa e mi contrista,
né di duol né di tema posso aitarme;

ché spesso nel suo volto veder parme
vera pietà con grave dolor mista,
et udir cose onde 'l cor fede acquista
che di gioia e di speme si disarme.

"Non ti soven di quella ultima sera"
dice ella "ch'i' lasciai li occhi tuoi molli,
e sforzata dal tempo me n'andai?

I' non tel potei dir allor né volli;
or tel dico per cosa esperta e vera:
non sperar di vedermi in terra mai".

CCL

In sleep my distant lady used to come,
consoling me with her angelic air,
but now she brings a sad foreboding there,
nor can the grief and dread be overcome;

for often in her countenance I seem
to see true pity blent with heavy care,
and hear those things that teach the heart despair,
since of all joy and hope it must disarm.

"Does our last evening not come back to you"
she says to me "and how your eyes were wet,
and how, compelled by time, I left you then?

I had no power nor wish to speak of it;
now can I say as something tried and true:
hope not to see me on this earth again."

IN MORTE DI
MADONNA LAURA

CCLXV

Aspro core e selvaggio e cruda voglia
in dolce, umile, angelica figura,
se l'impreso rigor gran tempo dura,
avran di me poco onorata spoglia;

ché quando nasce e mor fior, erba e foglia,
quando è 'l dì chiaro e quando è notte oscura,
piango ad ogni or. Ben ò di mia ventura,
di Madonna e d'Amore onde mi doglia.

Vivo sol di speranza, rimembrando
che poco umor già per continua prova
consumar vidi marmi e pietre salde:

non è sì duro cor che lagrimando,
pregando, amando, talor non si smova,
né sì freddo voler, che non si scalde.

CCLXV

Fierce heart and bitter, and most cruel will,
sweet, humble, and angelic to the sight,
if this first rigor last throughout the fight,
the honour of their trophies will be small;

for when grass, leaf, and flower spring and fall,
when daylight comes, and in the dark of night,
always I weep. Indeed I have the right
on Love, my fate, my lady thus to call.

I live on hope alone, remembering
how I have seen a little moisture prove
to wear down marble and the solid stone:

there cannot be a heart so hard that weeping,
praying, and loving sometime will not move,
nor yet a will so cold it cannot burn.

CCLXVII

Oimè il bel viso, oimè il soave sguardo,
oimè il leggiadro portamento altero!
Oimè il parlar ch'ogni aspro ingegno e fero
facevi umile ed ogni uom vil gagliardo!

Et oimè il dolce riso onde uscìo 'l dardo
di che morte, altro bene omai non spero!
Alma real, dignissima d'impero
se non fossi fra noi scesa sì tardo!

Per voi conven ch'io arda e 'n voi respire,
ch'i' pur fui vostro, e se di voi son privo
via men d'ogni sventura altra mi dole.

Di speranza m'empieste e di desire
quand'io parti' dal sommo piacer vivo:
ma 'l vento ne portava le parole.

CCLXVII

Alas the lovely face, the sweet regard,
alas the graceful bearing, proud and kind!
Alas the speech by which the rebel mind
was humbled and the coward given heart!

And O alas the smile that sent the dart
which now makes death the only hope I find!
Most royal soul, worthy to rule mankind
if you had not descended here so late!

Still must I breathe in you, still burn again,
since I was yours; and, robbed of you, the less
can any other sorrow grieve the mind.

With hope you filled me and desire when
I parted from the highest living bliss:
but all your words were taken by the wind.

CCLXXII

La vita fugge e non s'arresta un'ora
e la morte vien dietro a gran giornate
e le cose presenti e le passate
mi danno guerra, e le future ancora;

e 'l rimembrare e l'aspettar m'accora
or quinci or quindi, sì che 'n veritate,
se non ch'i' ò di me stesso pietate
i' sarei già di questi pensier fora.

Tornami avanti s'alcun dolce mai
ebbe 'l cor tristo, e poi da l'altra parte
veggio al mio navigar turbati i venti:

veggio fortuna in porto, e stanco omai
il mio nocchier, e rotte arbore e sarte,
e i lumi bei che mirar soglio, spenti.

CCLXXII

Life flees before, not stopping on the way,
and death with daylong marches follows fast,
and all things present join with all things past
and with the future to make war on me;

forethought and memory bring such dismay,
now one and now the other, that at last,
but for the piety that holds me fast,
I would already from such thoughts be free.

If any joy has lightened this sad heart,
it now returns to mind; then all around
I see the winds against my sailing bent:

I see a storm in port, and, tired out,
my pilot there, the mast and rigging down,
and the fair stars I contemplated spent.

CCLXXIX

Se lamentar augelli, o verdi fronde
mover soavemente a l'aura estiva,
o roco mormorar di lucide onde
s'ode d'una fiorita e fresca riva,

là 'v'io seggia d'amor pensoso e scriva;
lei che 'l ciel ne mostrò, terra n'asconde,
veggio et odo et intendo, ch'ancor viva
di sì lontano a' sospir miei risponde:

"Deh perché innanzi 'l tempo ti consume?"
mi dice con pietate "a che pur versi
degli occhi tristi un doloroso fiume?

Di me non pianger tu, che' miei dì fersi
morendo eterni, e ne l'interno lume,
quando mostrai de chiuder, gli occhi apersi".

CCLXXIX

If the lament of birds, or the green leaves
in summer breezes softly quivering,
or the hoarse murmur of translucent waves,
are heard on some fresh bank where flowers spring,

and where I sit and write the thought love brings;
then she whom heaven showed and earth receives
I see and hear, and know that ever living
she answers from afar the heart that grieves.

"Ah why untimely wear away the years?"
she says with pitying voice, "why shed
from sorrowing eyes this bitter flood of tears?

Weep not for me, know that my days were made
in death eternal; when I closed my eyes,
towards the inner light they opened wide."

CCXCII

Gli occhi di ch'io parlai sì caldamente,
e le braccia e le mani e i piedi e 'l viso
che m'avean sì da me stesso diviso
e fatto singular da l'altra gente;

le crespe chiome d'or puro lucente
e 'l lampeggiar de l'angelico riso
che solean fare in terra un paradiso,
poca polvere son che nulla sente;

et io pur vivo, onde mi doglio e sdegno,
rimaso senza 'l lume ch'amai tanto
in gran fortuna e 'n disarmato legno.

Or sia qui fine al mio amoroso canto,
secca è la vena de l'usato ingegno
e la cetera mia rivolta in pianto.

CCXCII

The eyes I spoke of once in words that burn,
the arms and hands and feet and lovely face
that took me from myself for such a space
of time and marked me out from other men;

the waving hair of unmixed gold that shone,
the smile that flashed with the angelic rays
that used to make this earth a paradise,
are now a little dust, all feeling gone;

and yet I live, grief and disdain to me,
left where the light I cherished never shows,
in fragile bark on the tempestuous sea.

Here let my loving song come to a close,
the vein of my accustomed art is dry,
and this, my lyre, turned at last to tears.

CCXCIII

S'io avesse pensato che sì care
fossin le voci de' sospir miei in rima,
fatte l'avrei dal sospirar mio prima
in numero più spesse, in stil più rare;

morta colei che mi facea parlare
e che si stava de' pensier miei in cima,
non posso, e non ò più sì dolce lima,
rime aspre e fosche far soavi e chiare.

E certo ogni mio studio in quel tempo era
pur di sfogare il doloroso core
in qualche modo, non d'acquistar fama;

pianger cercai, non già del pianto onore:
or vorrei ben piacer, ma quella altera
tacito stanco dopo sé mi chiama.

CCXCIII

If I had ever reckoned that so dear
would be the sighs that in these rhymes resound,
from the first sigh I would have made them sound
in greater numbers and in style more rare;

since she is dead who made me speak so fair,
and who alone amid my thoughts stood crowned,
I cannot hope, the file no more is found,
to make the rough dark verses smooth and clear.

Indeed my only study at that time
was all to give the sorrowing heart relief
in some poor fashion; fame was not the spur.

My grief sought tears, not honour for my grief:
now would I wish to please; but she, sublime,
beckons me, mute and weary, after her.

CCCII

Levommi il mio penser in parte ov'era
quella ch'io cerco e non ritrovo in terra;
ivi, fra lor che 'l terzo cerchio serra,
la rividi più bella e meno altera.

Per man mi prese e disse "In questa spera
sarai ancor meco, se 'l desir non erra:
i' so' colei che ti diè tanta guerra
e compie' mia giornata inanzi sera.

Mio ben non cape in intelletto umano:
te solo aspetto, e quel che tanto amasti
e là giuso è rimaso, il mio bel velo".

Deh perché tacque ed allargò la mano?
ch'al suon de' detti sì pietosi e casti
poco mancò ch'io non rimasi in cielo.

CCCII

My thoughts had lifted me to where she stood
whom I still seek and find on earth no more;
among the souls that the third circle bore,
she came with greater beauty and less pride.

She took my hand and said: "If hope can guide,
you will again be with me in this sphere:
for I am she who gave you so much war
and closed my day before the eventide.

No human mind can understand my bliss:
you I await and what you loved so much,
the veil I left below where now it lies."

Why did she loose my hand? why did she cease?
for at that holy and unsullied speech
I almost could have stayed in Paradise.

CCCX

Zefiro torna e 'l bel tempo rimena
e i fiori e l'erbe, sua dolce famiglia,
e garrir Progne e pianger Filomena,
e primavera candida e vermiglia;

ridono i prati e 'l ciel si rasserena,
Giove s'allegra di mirar sua figlia,
l'aria e l'acqua e la terra è d'amor piena,
ogni animal d'amar si riconsiglia.

Ma per me, lasso, tornano i più gravi
sospiri, che del cor profondo tragge
quella ch'al ciel se ne portò le chiavi,

e cantar augelletti e fiorir piagge
e 'n belle donne oneste atti soavi
sono un deserto e fere aspre e selvagge.

CCCX

Zephyr returns, fair weather in his train,
and flowers and grass, and all his gentle brood,
and Procne's chirp and Philomel's sad strain,
and spring in scarlet and in white renewed;

the sky grows clear and smiling is the plain,
Jove on his daughter looks in happy mood,
love fills the water, air, and earth again,
and every creature finds love's counsel good.

To me, alas, return more heavy sighs,
drawn from the heart in that profound distress
by one who took its keys to paradise;

and birdsong and the hillside's flowered dress
and ladies in their motion sweet and wise
seem savage beasts that roam a wilderness.

CCCXI

Quel rosignuol che sì soave piagne
forse suoi figli o sua cara consorte
di dolcezza empie il cielo e le campagne
con tante note sì pietose e scorte,

e tutta notte par che m'accompagne
e mi rammente la mia dura sorte,
ch'altri che me non ò di chi mi lagne
ché 'n dee non credev'io regnasse Morte.

O che lieve è inganar chi s'assecura!
Que' duo bei lumi assai più che 'l sol chiari
chi pensò mai veder far terra oscura?

Or cognosco io che mia fera ventura
vuol che vivendo e lagrimando impari
come nulla qua giù diletta e dura!

CCCXI

That nightingale, who now so softly mourns
perhaps his children or his precious mate,
with sweetness floods the heavens and the plains,
in notes so full of sorrow and of art;

and through the night I seem to hear his strain
recalling to the mind my cruel fate;
for only of myself can I complain,
that goddesses could die I knew too late.

How easy to deceive the man who trusts!
Those two fair lights, much brighter than the sun,
who thought to see them darkened in the dust?

But now I know my destiny insists
that living thus and weeping I should learn
how nothing here can both delight and last.

CCCXLVI

Li angeli eletti e l'anime beate
cittadine del cielo, il primo giorno
che Madonna passò, le fur intorno
piene di meraviglia e di pietate.

"Che luce è questa e qual nova beltate"
dicean tra lor "per ch'abito sì adorno
dal mondo errante a quest'alto soggiorno
non salì mai in tutta questa etate?"

Ella contenta aver cangiato albergo
si paragona pur coi più perfetti,
e parte ad or ad or si volge a tergo

mirando s'io la seguo, e par ch'aspetti:
ond'io voglie e pensier tutti al ciel ergo
perch'i' l'odo pregar pur ch'i' m'affretti.

CCCXLVI

On my dear lady's passing, that first day,
the chosen angels and the spirits blest,
the citizens of heaven, came and pressed
with wonder and respect about her way.

"What light and what new loveliness" they say
"for never has a form so finely dressed
mounted from errant earth to this high rest
while all the present age has passed away?"

And she, contented to have changed her state,
among the perfect ones stands no less rare,
and often turning back she seems to wait

to see if I am following her there:
so that to heaven I raise all hope and thought,
hearing her bid me hasten in her prayer.

CCCLXII

Volo con l'ali de' pensieri al cielo
sì spesse volte, che quasi un di loro
esser mi par ch'àn ivi il suo tesoro
lasciando in terra lo squarciato velo.

Talor mi trema 'l cor d'un dolce gelo,
udendo lei per ch'io mi discoloro
dirmi: "Amico, or t'am'io ed or t'onoro
perch'à' i costumi variati e 'l pelo".

Menami al suo Signor; allor m'inchino
pregando umilemente che consenta
ch'i' stia a veder e l'uno e l'altro volto.

Responde: "Egli è ben fermo il tuo destino,
e per tardar ancor vent'anni o trenta
parrà a te troppo e non fia però molto".

CCCLXII

I fly on wings of thought to paradise
so often that I almost seem to enter
the company that there finds all its treasure,
leaving on earth the veil that shattered lies.

At times a trembling and sweet chill will rise
within my heart as she who drains my colour
says: "Now, my friend, I give you love and honour,
since you have changed your skin and changed your ways."

She leads me to her Lord, and there I bow,
humbly praying that he will let me stay
to look on his and also on her face.

And he replies: "Your fate is certain now,
and though some twenty, thirty years' delay
seem long to you, it is a little space."

CCCLXIV

Tennemi Amor anni ventuno ardendo
lieto nel foco e nel duol pien di speme;
poi che Madonna e 'l mio cor seco inseme
saliro al ciel, dieci altri anni piangendo;

omai son stanco e mia vita reprendo
di tanto error, che di vertute il seme
à quasi spento, e le mie parti estreme,
alto Dio, a te devotamente rendo,

pentito e tristo de' miei sì spesi anni:
che spender si deveano in miglior uso,
in cercar pace ed in fuggir affanni.

Signor che 'n questo carcer m'ài rinchiuso
tramene salvo da li eterni danni,
ch'i' conosco 'l mio fallo e non lo scuso.

CCCLXIV

For twenty-one long years Love made me burn,
glad in the fire, hopeful in my pain;
my lady took my heart to heaven's domain,
and still he gave me ten more years to mourn;

now I am weary, and my life I spurn
for so much error that has almost slain
the seed of virtue, and what years remain,
high God, to you devoutly I return,

contrite and sad for every misspent year,
for time I should have put to better use
in seeking peace and shunning passions here.

Lord, having pent me in this prison close,
from everlasting torment draw me clear;
I know my fault and offer no excuse.

CCCLXV

I' vo piangendo i miei passati tempi
i quai posi in amar cosa mortale,
senza levarmi a volo, abbiend'io l'ale
per dar forse di me non bassi esempi.

Tu che vedi i miei mali indegni et empi,
Re del cielo, invisibile, immortale,
soccorri a l'alma disviata e frale,
e 'l suo defetto di tua grazia adempi;

sì che, s'io vissi in guerra ed in tempesta,
mora in pace ed in porto, e se la stanza
fu vana, almen sia la partita onesta.

A quel poco di viver che m'avanza
ed al morir degni esser tua man presta:
tu sai ben che 'n altrui non ò speranza.

CCCLXV

I keep lamenting over days gone by,
the time I spent loving a mortal thing,
with no attempt to soar, although my wing
might give no mean example in the sky.

You that my foul unworthy sins descry,
unseen and everlasting, heaven's King,
succour my soul, infirm and wandering,
and what is lacking let your grace supply;

so if I lived in tempest and in war,
I die in port and peace; however vain
the stay, at least the parting may be fair.

Now in the little life that still remains
and at my death may your quick hand be near:
in others, you well know, my hope is gone.

NOTES

Few volumes of poetry have been annotated as thoroughly as the *Canzoniere*. In the sixteenth century editors such as Filelfo, Squarciafico, Gesualdo, and Vellutello produced a mass of commentary that can only be compared to the academic industry of our own times. Faced by this embarrassment of riches, I have tried to keep my own notes fairly simple, drawing attention to my own choices as a translator only where these seemed significant or debatable. I hope that some reference to Renaissance translations will prove of interest to students of English poetry.

I
1. 1. *rime sparse*. The poet regards his "scattered rhymes" as a collection of fragments (*Rerum vulgarium fragmenta*), but there is also the possibility that they are scattered through the world. The whole sonnet is, indeed, indicative of Petrarch's ambiguous attitude towards the *Canzoniere*: he deplores it as evidence of a "youthful error," but he still hopes to find readers.

There are anonymous Tudor translations in *Tottel's Miscellany* (1557) and in the Hill Manuscript (Add. MS. 36529, B.M.).

III
Petrarch first saw Laura at matins in the church of Saint Clare in Avignon on April 6, 1327. This was not the moveable feast of Good Friday, but, according to medieval calculations, the exact calendar anniversary of Christ's death.

There is an anonymous version in *Tottel's Miscellany*.

XIII
1. 12. *leggiadria*. A key word in Petrarch and one that makes the translator despair. At times it has the simple physical connotations of lightness and charm, but here the dominant suggestion is that of spiritual buoyancy. The reader will, I hope, stretch a point and allow "graceful" some theological overtones.

XVI

If the poet occasionally looks at other women, it is because he seeks in their faces some resemblance to Laura. He is like the pilgrim who travels to Rome to see the famous Veronica, the cloth on which Christ wiped his face and left his image.

XXI

1. 12. *poria smarrire il suo natural corso*. An obscure line which Carducci and Ferrari read as meaning that the poet will die. The verb *smarrire*, however, would suggest sin rather than death.

See Sir Thomas Wyatt's "How oft have I, my dear and cruel foe," and an anonymous version in *The Phoenix Nest* (1593).

XXII

1. 25. In the *Timaeus* Plato teaches that the soul leaves its native star when it is sent by Nature to occupy the body. At death, if it has lived well, it returns to its star again.

1. 26. *amorosa selva*. The "lovers' wood" is the myrtle-grove assigned to unfortunate lovers in the Underworld. See Virgil, *Aeneid*, VI, 442–444.

11. 29–30. It is indicative of Petrarch's ease in handling the rigid sestina form that this is the only point where the syntax seems slightly awkward.

11. 34–36. A play on Laura's name. Daphne was saved from the advances of Apollo by being transformed into a laurel. On this rare occasion the physical desire becomes explicit.

XXXIV

Usually understood as referring to an illness of Laura, this is one of the so-called "Daphnean" poems where Laura is associated with Daphne, the laurel, the symbol of poetry. Apollo has a triple function here. As the lover of Daphne, he is bound to admire her reincarnation as Laura; as the sun-god, he will dispel the winter that affects her health; as protector of poets, he will share in Petrarch's wonder as she is transformed into the laurel of poetic achievement.

1. 2. *tesaliche onde*. The River Peneus in Thessaly where Apollo pursued Daphne.

1. 10. *vita acerba*. The "bitter life" when Apollo, exiled from Olympus, lived on earth as a shepherd.

126

1. 14. In Vatican MS. 3195 Petrarch has substituted *braccia* (arms) for the earlier *rami* (branches). Instead of simply seeing Laura/Daphne as a laurel, we assist at the moment of transformation.

XLIX

1. 11. *la mia pace*. Laura who alone can give him peace. See Wyatt's "Because I have thee still kept from lies and blame."

LII

The pastoral transformation of Laura into a shepherdess occurs nowhere else in the *Canzoniere*. Carducci and Ferrari suggest that, since the poem is a madrigal, Petrarch is being faithful to the supposed derivation of *madrigale* from *mandriale* (*mandria*, herd, flock).

1. 4. *cruda*. The adjective suggests not only immaturity, but also a toughness and severity that associates Laura with the harsh mountain climate. The English "raw" is inadequate, but it has some of the right connotations.

1. 6. *a l'aura*. The usual untranslatable play on Laura's name. I have taken the liberty of substituting one pun for another.

There is a version by Nicholas Yonge in *Musica Transalpina* (1588).

LXXIV

The syntax of the original sounds a good deal less fluid in English, partly because I have been forced to translate the infinitive *pensar* (1. 1.) with a noun.

11. 13-14. Two interpretations seem possible:
a) If it is a fault to write so much about you, love is to blame and not my art which is capable of handling other themes.
b) If these poems are unworthy of their subject, do not blame my art for being too weak, but my love for being too strong.

XC

Compare Virgil, *Aeneid*, I, 319-327.

CXXII

11. 5-6. The reference is to a Latin proverb, *vulpem pilum mutare non mores*, the fox can change his fur, not his ways.

1. 8. The shade of the passions is cast by the "heavy veil" of the body.

1. 14. *e quanto si convene*. Literally "as much as is fitting." Somewhat wryly Petrarch looks forward to a time when his love for Laura will be less intense and will allow him to contemplate her without any sense of guilt.

CXXVI

1. 1. The waters of the Sorgue in Vaucluse.

11. 7–9. Commentators have been unnecessarily puzzled here. The poet, in fact, recalls Laura in a number of different attitudes: bathing in the river, leaning against a tree, and sitting on the ground so that the gown which covers her breast also covers the grass and flowers.

11. 36–39. Bosco points out that heaven will be impressed not by Laura's sorrow or piety, but by the sweetness of her sighs and the elegance of her gestures. Even the intercession of the living for the dead is seen in aesthetic terms.

CXXIX

11. 17–19. The subject of *gira* is *penser novo*, not *mia donna*. Laura does not make fun of the poet's sufferings.

1. 48. *adombra*. More than "shadow forth" this suggests the conscious chiaroscuro of the painter, thus continuing the artist metaphor introduced in the previous stanza.

11. 51–52. The contrast is probably between the stone effigy on a tomb (*pietra morta*) and the natural stone (*pietra viva*) on which the poet sits. Having transformed so many shapes into Laura's image, the poet now becomes an image himself. This reading is confirmed by the last line of the poem.

11. 66–72. The envoi sends the poem to join the poet's heart which is with Laura beyond the Alps. For once I have attempted to translate the pun on Laura's name.

CXXXII

1. 2. *che cosa e quale*. I have simplified here. Petrarch, probably thinking of some scholastic distinction, asks two questions: what and which?

This sonnet and CXXXIV provide the most striking examples of Petrarchan antitheses and were widely imitated. For English versions see Chaucer (the "Canticus Troili" in *Troilus and Criseyde*), the Hill Manuscript, Thomas Watson (*Hekatompathia*, 1582), and *Davison's Rhapsody* (1602).

CXXXIV

See Wyatt's "I find no peace and all my war is done" and also a version by Thomas Watson in *Hekatompathia.*

CXL

The only sonnet to be translated by both Wyatt ("The long love that in my thought doth harbour") and Surrey ("Love that doth reign and live within my thought").

CLIX

11. 1-2. It is difficult in English to bring out the correct Platonic resonance of *idea*. My translation of *esempio* as "the perfect model" is no more than a gesture in this direction.

1. 8. *la somma.* Commentators debate whether this means "the sum of her virtues" or "her highest virtue." In the latter case it would be Laura's chastity that is guilty of the poet's death.

There is a version by Nicholas Yonge in *Musica Transalpina.*

CLXIV

1. 12. *giunga a riva.* At the risk of obscurity, I have chosen to preserve the image rather than to paraphrase it as "come to an end."

See Surrey's "Alas, so all things now do hold their peace" and versions by the Scottish Petrarchists, William Fowler and William Drummond of Hawthornden.

CLXIX

See Wyatt's "Such vain thought as wonted to mislead me."

CLXXX

1. 7. *l'aurea fronde.* Literally "the golden bough," the passport of Aeneas through the underworld. But there is also the customary play on Laura and the laurel, hence my expansion of the phrase.

11. 10-11. The Po flows eastward towards the rising sun, but away from the "greater splendor" of Laura in the west at Avignon.

1. 12. River-gods are traditionally represented with horns.

CLXXXI

A birdcatching metaphor where Laura's hair, voice, and eyes become the net, the imitated birdcall, and the mirror in the trap. The "dear evergreen" is, of course, the laurel.

CXC

This sonnet has given rise to a number of interpretations. For some early commentators the chain around the hind's neck indicated Laura's married state, for others her chastity. The poem has also been read as a premonition of Laura's death, the chain in this case being symbolic of her ultimate union with God.

1. 3. *fra due riviere.* Possibly a reference to the Sorgue and the Durance in Vaucluse.

11. 9–12. Petrarch is using the legend which tells how, some three hundred years after Caesar's death, a hind was found with a collar bearing the words, *Noli me tangere, Cesaris sum.*

Wyatt adapts this sonnet to his own very different purposes in "Whoso list to hunt." Spenser adds his own variation to the theme in "Like as a huntsman" (*Amoretti*, LXVII).

CXCIX

It is through poems like this and CCI that Petrarch remains a diffused influence even when the love-lyric is reduced to an elegant compliment. The whole situation smacks of the drawing room.

See the opening stanzas of Wyatt's "O goodly hand."

CCI

1. 2. The glove of CXCIX which the poet now regrets having returned.

CCXXIV

A popular sonnet in the English Renaissance. See Wyatt's "If amour's faith," Samuel Daniel's "If that a loyal heart" (*Delia*, XV), and an anonymous version in the Hill Manuscript.

CCXXXIV

The forerunner of many Renaissance sonnets addressed to the bed or the room. Compare Wyatt's "The restful place, reviver of my smart," and Sir Philip Sidney's "Ah bed, the field where joy's peace some do see" (*Astrophil and Stella*, XCVIII)

CCXLV

At least two Renaissance commentators (Squarciafico and Antonio da Tempo) relate that this episode actually occurred in the garden of a Florentine monastery known as "Paradiso." There is no evidence for this pleasant legend, but it provides an early example of the perennial urge to discover the "true story" of the *Canzoniere*. Perhaps only Shakespeare's *Sonnets* have been subjected to more biographical speculation.

CCXLVIII

11. 1–2. *natura e 'l ciel tra noi.* Heaven is the ultimate cause which animates, and Nature the proximate cause which provides the material form. This opening inspired many imitations, a celebrated example being Sidney's "Who will in fairest book of Nature know" (*Astrophil and Stella*, LXXI). See also Watson's "Who list to view Dame Nature's cunning skill" in *Hekatompathia*.

CCL

One of a group of sonnets dealing with the premonition of Laura's imminent death.

CCLXV

Obviously concerned with a living woman, despite its position among the poems *in morte*.

CCLXVII

Generally assumed to reflect Petrarch's first anguish on hearing of Laura's death. The news reached him at Parma on May 19, 1348. In his copy of Virgil, Petrarch wrote:

> Laura, illustrious through her own virtues, and long famed through my verses, first appeared to my eyes in my youth, in the year of our Lord 1327, on the sixth day of April, in the church of St. Clare in Avignon, at matins; and in the same city, also on the sixth day of April, at the same first hour, but in the year 1348, the light of her life was withdrawn from the light of day. (trans. Ernest Hatch Wilkins)

The evidence suggests that we have no good reason to doubt the astonishing coincidence of dates.

CCLXXII

1. 7. *di me stesso pietate.* Not sentimental self-pity, but the piety that restrains him from suicide and damnation.

11. 9–14. Commentators spend a good deal of energy in explicating the details of Petrarch's marine imagery. For our purposes it is enough to know that the pilot is Reason and the "fair stars" the eyes of Laura.

CCLXXIX
See William Fowler's "She whom I loved."

CCXCII
1. 14. Job, xxx, 31: *cithara mea versa est in luctum*.

The octave is imitated by Drummond ("Those eyes, those sparkling sapphires of delight") and also by Sir Walter Ralegh ("Those eyes which set my fancy on a fire").

CCCII
1. 3. *terzo cerchio*. The third circle, the sphere of Venus assigned to great lovers in the *Paradiso*.

1. 8. *inanzi sera*. A reference to Laura's untimely death.

1. 11. *il mio bel velo*. The body. Laura awaits two separate events: the death of Petrarch and the Resurrection of the Body.

The influence of this poem and of all the dream-poems *in morte* can be felt in Milton's "Methought I saw my late espousèd saint."

CCCX
A very popular sonnet during the English Renaissance. There are versions by Nicholas Yonge (*Musica Transalpina*) and Thomas Watson (*Italian Madrigals Englished*, 1590). Surrey's "The soote season" and Drummond's "Sweet Spring, thou turn'st" are variations on the same theme.

CCCXI
In Petrarch's treatment of the conventional nightingale there is a distinct echo of Virgil, *Georgics*, IV, 511–515.

Thomas Morley has an unusually literal version in *Madrigals to Five Voices* (1598).

CCCXLVI
The arrival of the lady among the blessed is in the tradition of the *Dolce Stil Novo*. We think of Cino da Pistoia consoling Dante for the death of Beatrice:

Ché Dio, nostro signore,
volle di lei, com'avea l'angiol detto,
fare il cielo perfetto.
Per nova cosa ogni santo la mira,
ed ella sta davanti alla Salute.
ed invèr lei parla onne Virtute.

For God, our Lord, wished with her, as the angel had said, to make heaven perfect. As a wondrous creature every saint gazes upon her, and she stands before her Saviour, and, in truth, she expresses every virtue.

Laura passes amid the admiring looks and comments of the heavenly crowd, glancing back occasionally to see if the poet is following her. Despite the rarefied atmosphere, she has never been so convincingly feminine.

1. 10. *si paragona pur coi più perfetti.* Literally "she compares herself even with the most perfect ones." But we must resist the temptation to read in this a hint of female vanity. Laura takes her rightful place among the elect, but there is no competition in heaven.

CCCLXII

1. 3. *ch'àn ivi il suo tesoro.* Matthew, vi, 19: "Lay up for yourselves treasure in Heaven."

1. 8. A variation of the proverb quoted in CXXII. The poet's skin (or hair) has changed with age; unlike the fox, he has also changed his ways.

1. 11. *l'uno e l'altro volto.* God's face and Laura's.

CCCLXIV

Petrarch sums up the basic chronology of the *Canzoniere*: the meeting with Laura in 1327, her death in 1348, and the final renunciation which, on the evidence of this sonnet, came in 1358.

CCCLXV

The last sonnet, but not the last poem in the *Canzoniere*, which concludes with a canzone to the Virgin.

11. 3-4. The humility of the recantation is rendered more poignant by this lingering touch of human pride. Love for the "mortal thing" has been an obstacle to salvation, but there is also the explicit regret that it has prevented him from demonstrating his true worth in the eyes of the world.

The Hill Manuscript contains two versions of this sonnet.

CHRONOLOGY

1304 Arezzo, July 20, birth of Francesco Petrarca (Petrarch), son of exiled Florentine notary.

1311 With family at Pisa; probably sees Dante.

1312 Father moves to Avignon, seat of Papal Court; Petrarch with family at Carpentras fifteen miles away.

1316 Begins study of law at Montpellier.

1320 At University of Bologna where his studies are interrupted by student riots.

1326 Abandons study of law. On death of father returns to Avignon and begins ecclesiastical career, eventually taking minor orders.

1327 April 6, in church of Saint Clare, sees Laura, probably Laura de Noves, wife of Hugues de Sade.

1330 In Gascony with Bishop Giacomo Colonna. On return to Avignon enters service of bishop's brother, Cardinal Giovanni Colonna. Earliest poems in *Canzoniere* date from this period.

1333 Travels in France, Germany, Flanders. Discovers Cicero's *Pro Archia*. Receives copy of Saint Augustine's *Confessions*.

1336 Climbs Mont Ventoux. Leaves for Rome, arriving January, 1337.

1337 Retires to Vaucluse. Birth of illegitimate son Giovanni.

1338 Begins *De viris illustribus*, Latin epic *Africa*, and perhaps *Trionfi*.

1341 Coronation as Poet Laureate in Rome. Selects and orders Italian lyrics, possibly a hundred in all, the first form of *Canzoniere*.

1342 Attempts to learn Greek. Begins *Secretum*, an intimate confessional work in the form of a prose dialogue with Saint Augustine.

1343 Embassy for Pope Clement VI at court of Naples. Birth of illegitimate daughter Francesca.

1344 At Parma where he begins *Liber rerum memorandarum*.

1345 Leaves Parma. Discovers Cicero's letters *Ad Atticum*. Returns to Vaucluse.

1346 Begins *De vita solitaria* and *Bucolicum carmen*.

1347 Leaves for Rome to salute new leader Cola di Rienzi in the hope that he will restore the Roman Republic. Stops at Genoa when he hears of Cola's setbacks.

1348 At Parma and Verona. Death of Laura.

1349 Prepares second form of *Canzoniere*, probably about a hundred and thirty poems. Starts to collect his letters.

1350 In Verona, Mantua, Rome, Arezzo, Florence. Cola di Rienzi imprisoned.

1351 In Padua. Refuses Boccaccio's invitation to lecture in Florence. Returns to Vaucluse.

1352 Works on *Trionfi*.

1353 Moves to Milan where he stays eight years as guest of the Visconti.

1354 Begins *De remediis utriusquae fortunae*. Cola di Rienzi killed by Roman mob.

1356 Embassy to Imperial Court at Prague. Releases *De vita solitaria* and *De otio religioso*. Begins work on third form of *Canzoniere*.

1357 Releases *Bucolicum carmen*.

1358 Completes third form of *Canzoniere*, now containing one hundred and seventy poems.

1359 Receives visit from Boccaccio, who stays nearly a month. They discuss the merits of Dante. Work starts on fourth form of *Canzoniere* (the Chigi version).

1361 Mission to Paris. Returns to Milan, moves to Padua, and finally to Venice. At about this time completes Chigi version of *Canzoniere*, now containing two hundred and fifteen poems.

1365 Arranges his letters.

1366 Releases *De remediis*. Begins work on fifth and final form of *Canzoniere*.

1367 *De sui ipsius et multorum ignorantia*, an invective against four Aristotelians.

1368 In Padua. Visit from Boccaccio.

1370 Retires to country house at Arquà, ten miles from Padua. Makes will. *Canzoniere* now contains about three hundred poems.

1374 In January and February works on *Trionfo dell'eternità*. Revision of *Canzoniere* continues. Final version, substantially complete, has three hundred and sixty-six poems. Petrarch dies at Arquà, July 18.

INDEX

OF FIRST LINES IN ITALIAN TEXT

137